Pressed
Wild Flower
Pictures

By the same author (with Margaret Kennedy Scott) and published by Batsford
Making Pressed Flower Pictures (paperback, 1979)
Pressed Flowers through the Seasons (cased, 1983)

Pressed Wild Flower Pictures

Mary Beazley

B.T. Batsford Ltd   London

Photographs by Julyan Rawlings

© Mary Beazley 1985

First published 1985

ISBN 0 7134 4614 5

Typeset by Servis Filmsetting Ltd, Manchester
and printed in Great Britain by
Anchor Brendon Ltd Tiptree, Essex
for the publishers
B.T. Batsford Ltd
4 Fitzhardinge Street
London W1H 0AH

Contents

Introduction

One must begin at the beginning in everything and in learning about wild flowers time spent in the countryside should be the starting point. If you enjoy walking for its own sake or simply look forward to picnicking on holiday, then you will meet flowers every year as old friends and you will wonder what their names are and perhaps wish that you could distinguish between one variety and another.

This book is intended to bring up to date the old Victorian craft or art of pressing wild flowers. It will show you that if you follow a pattern of pressing them throughout the year, they will become so familiar that identification will seem a natural extension of your interest. The book will help you to learn about many common wild plants; it will guide you on how to press material from them and will show you how to use it in delicately arranged designs. By the end of the year you will have a charming collection of flowers and will also have acquired a surprising amount of interesting knowledge, and perhaps noted this down beside the flowers. You can complete an album, filling every page with a different group of flowers or you can frame the designs and start a small collection of flower pictures.

Hobbies and leisure interests, as they are called, flourish nowadays but anything remotely bracketed with botany seems destined for neglect. The idea that you must be able to cope with Latin classification needs to be quickly dispelled; this is not essential to the beginner and it is a sad fact that many a good, solid book on British botany has claimed early victims by first bewildering and then boring them to death. Linnaeus – admirable Swede and botanist that he was – has reigned too long over the level of wild flower study where the followers are enthusiasts, not botanists.

Before the turn of the century, people were far more familiar with the names and habits of our wild plants than most of us are today. The tradition of herbal medicine was still a factor in their lives and they passed on to their children what was common knowledge; men and women mentioned wild flowers quite naturally in their letters and diaries and, when they travelled abroad, were able to identify the flowers they found and compare them botanically with the ones in England. We seem to have allowed this gentle tradition of rural knowledge almost to peter out – possibly the motor car rushes past the hedgerows too quickly; perhaps the grass verges where the wild flowers used to grow are too often trimmed and tidied and our eye has become accustomed to the municipal taste. Arguably we can be excused for swallowing our penicillin in preference to a syrup of coltsfoot *Tussilaga farfara* without question but, whatever the reasons, the fact remains that many people do not know one wild flower from another.

There are 33 flowers featured in this book, although general mention is made of many others; most of them are widespread over the British Isles and can be easily found. The selection covers fully not only the four seasons of the year but also the four natural habitats of woodland, fields and their hedgerows, moorland and the coast. The different shades and colours of our common flowers are all represented, from the strong scarlet of poppies and the purple of heather to the unusual green and cream of white bryony and traveller's joy. There are small grasses, ferns and sorrels used to augment the leaves of the selected plants in some of the mixed flower designs but these are chosen purely for their shape and colour and have not been specifically named. Some of the flowers feature in their own arrangements, each showing the natural habit of growth and line of the plant, while the remaining flowers are grouped so as to make colourful and artistic pictures.

There is advice on pressing all the flowers and there are outline drawings of many of the designs together with simple instructions on how to assemble them. Each of the life-size drawings shows clearly the natural lines of growth as well as the basic outline of the dried flower *as it will be* after pressing. (This will sometimes vary slightly from the three-dimensional appearance of the fresh flower and also as it may be depicted in an illustrated book of wild flowers.) You will discover that your own pressed flowers and leaves, paper-thin and brittle when you lift them from the press, will closely resemble those in the outline drawing and so can be matched against them. You can cover the outline drawing in the book with a semi-transparent skin of paper or fabric and, with it fixed firmly down over the illustration, you will have a pattern to follow, a guide for the placing and fixing down of your own pressed material. Your flowers and leaves may differ slightly in size and you may have to adapt your stems or accept the modified angle of a half-opened bud, but basically the flowers always follow their own characteristic pattern of growth and they will oblige you. It is, in fact, difficult to succeed in pressing a flower crookedly, for the natural bend of a stem or curl of a petal will normally survive the press. Some flowers not included in this book (and they are in the minority) are impossible to press at all without recourse to scissors and a little cheating – the most casual glance at a large prickly thistle will persuade you that it qualifies for membership of this group!

Every flower chosen for this book is featured in one of the designs and drawings, and each has accompanying details of where and when it can be found and simple points to help you identify it. There is also advice about picking and pressing on neighbouring pages and notes of any change in colour to be expected.

The craft of pressing, trimming and handling the wild flowers, their leaves and buds, curly tendrils and even some of the seed-heads, will train your fingers to greater neatness and control, while the artistic side of making flower designs will increase an appreciation of colour and shape, a critical eye for perfection and a deeper pleasure in these fragile inhabitants of the countryside.

The equipment is inexpensive and simple. You will need a small flower press and a quantity of blotting paper, scissors, a little fabric, adhesive and a small pair of tweezers. You will find further advice about these basic requirements in the alphabetically arranged section on pp. 23–7, and there are complete instructions in the following chapters on how to press the flowers and leaves which are used in the designs throughout this book.

The first design of the year is of snowdrops and this could be an excellent starting point for your flower study. Look at the drawing carefully and read the advice as to where and when you should look for this early spring flower. Make sure that you know how many flowers you are going to need for the picture and then cut from the plants accordingly. Follow the notes on how to press snowdrops and by the middle of April you should be ready to assemble your first design. Advice on trimming and fixing down your pressed material is given in the section on p. 28 headed 'Making the designs'. There are suggestions here, too, about mounting the finished picture as well as simple advice about protecting it against fading. Get into the habit of keeping the small flowers and pieces of pressed material which are left over from your designs – you will find them very useful if you decide to make Christmas cards for your family and friends at the end of the year.

You will have noticed that the snowdrop is also called *Galanthus nivalis*. All flowering plants still have the old Latin names as well as the ordinary British names to describe them. The Latin ones are kept because it makes a common language, amongst other things, for flower lovers all over the world. A *Lotus corniculatus*, for example, means the same flower to a German as it does to a Greek, or to us. We know it as bird's foot trefoil, that small, yellow summer flower that also rejoices in a variety of local country names – 'eggs and bacon', 'fingers and thumbs' and 'Tom thumb'. It is used in Figure 22 and you will find the Latin name included in the description of the flower. If you find enjoyment in learning about wild flowers from this book and want to discover more about them or about other varieties, then familiarity with the Latin names will stand you in good stead. There is more detailed explanation and information in Chapter 7 which will tell you about the flower families to which the chosen flowers belong. You will find it helpful in learning about wild flowers to have the assistance of a simple reference book on the wild flowers of Britain; there is a short list of well-tried books on p. 118, and the *Oxford Book of Wild Flowers*, which follows a basic grouping of flowers by colour, is a particularly good one to start with. Some of the wild flowers used in this book are not indigenous to this country and are even now labelled as 'garden escapees' by some botanists, but once these flowers have become naturalised and survive and increase in their new habitat, most authors of wild flower books include them in their pages. Wild flowers from other parts of the world can be pressed and preserved and, towards the end of the book, you will find advice about collecting flowers while on holidays.

Your first year spent in finding out about wild flowers will give you a great deal of fun, and the charm of the subject will probably convert you into becoming a champion for their protection. They badly need enthusiasts and devotees who will object to the unthinking use of weedkillers and the unnecessary cutting of road verges before the seeds scatter. (Present policy tends to eliminate every flower on motorway verges except the ubiquitous dandelions, and they seem to flourish!) The worst assaults on wild flowers come through ignorance, and the best safeguard is to swell the number of people who love them and who understand their short life-cycle.

A few flowers are already very rare indeed and many others are becoming less common; they all need to be protected by commonsense as well as by laws. When you are collecting flowers for pressing, never pick indiscriminately – one flower from one plant is a good rule to follow – and never pick at all when there is only a single plant in the vicinity. One less flower means one less seed-head for the following year.

1 Wild Flowers

a wild rose

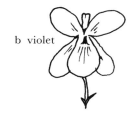

b violet

c meadow sweet

d bird's foot trefoil

1

The most striking thing about a flowering plant is usually the colour of its petals, but to describe it solely as one with 'a lot of little yellow flowers' would be pointless so far as recognition goes – this might as well apply to a celandine as to a ragwort. There are well over 100 fairly common wild plants in the British Isles which have yellow flowers, and to depend on colour alone for identification would be completely inadequate. Size, shape, texture, scent and style of growth, as well as the colour, all play a part, and in order that words of identification should not be ambiguous, the various parts of the plants as well as certain descriptive adjectives have been defined concisely as to their botanical meaning. Over the years, botanists and indeed all lovers of wild flowers have availed themselves of this technical and descriptive language when they have needed to be precise about any particular plant, using as little or as much of it as required, and in subsequent chapters of this book you will find that this useful vocabulary is sometimes employed to describe the plants. There is a list of these words at the end of the book on p. 100–1.

How and why plants grow in the way that they do, how they have evolved their own highly individualistic manner of growth, and how they have adapted to meet their often unlovely and overcrowded habitats are things of great interest; but this is the study of botanists and it must be enough for us that we should understand the simple fact that nature is always functional. There is always a reason behind a particular pattern of growth and often an ulterior motive in spectacular beauty of colour and shape of a flower. The brightness of some blossoms, for example, especially attracts the insect which pollinates them best and to that insect the same bright shade signals the nectar he most enjoys. It is a mutual dependence, finely worked out and one which, on the whole, succeeds.

For the flower, the protection of its petals when they are in the bud is paramount, and the covering sheath of sepals is usually tough and fits tightly together around the incredibly delicate and tightly convoluted infant petals. Only when the petals are fully swollen and developed will the sepals break open, and then the bud will have become a flower. (Sometimes the sepals themselves show both a colour and form which are usually only present in true petals. Figures 2b and 2c show the flowers of traveller's joy and wood anemone where the apparent 'petals' are in fact the sepals.)

The plant must reproduce itself, and nearly all have a system of fertilisation which requires the pollen produced by the male part of the flower, called the stamens, to be transferred to a pistil, or female part, which produces the seeds. Insects, particularly the honey-bee, fly from flower to similar flower in search of nectar; they unconsciously disturb the ripe pollen from the tops of the stamens and it is brushed off on to the fluffy body of the bee and finally deposited on the sticky tip of a stigma. Once fertilisation is completed, the seed in the ovary at the base of the flower begins to grow. Sometimes the pollen from one species of flower is carried to another – this is called cross-pollination – and a resulting plant will show characteristics of both parents.

The seeds, like the petals in the bud, must be protected while they are maturing and the outside case of the seed container is usually hard enough to withstand rain, wind and cold weather. Only when the seed is fully ripe, scattered and lying on the ground and encouraged by warmth from the sun and moisture from rain or dew, will it break open, put down a root and begin to grow. The first small stem and folded leaf which the seed puts up is called the shoot and, given the right weather conditions, it will grow quickly. Other types of plants employ different methods of multiplying themselves: some put out long roots under-

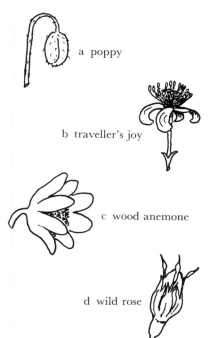

a poppy

b traveller's joy

c wood anemone

d wild rose

2

3 A collection of seed-heads and autumn foliage set in a deep frame. Included is material from cowparsley, traveller's joy, bog cotton, rosebay willowherb, vetch, wild strawberry, bramble, oak and beech.

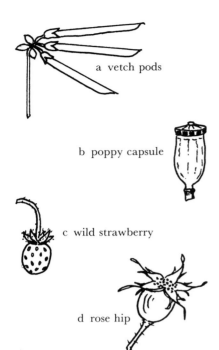

a vetch pods

b poppy capsule

c wild strawberry

d rose hip

4

ground which turn up into the light and start another plant; some put out runners along the surface of the ground – the strawberry is a good example of this – while a third group, which stores nourishment every year in bulbs or corms, is able to produce miniature ones which will grow into independent plants.

Seeds are held in various types of cases or fruits by the plant until they are ripe and ready for dispersal, and this process of maturation can take many weeks. Figure 4 shows some of the varieties of shapes of plant pods and capsules that can be found; some of the systems which they employ for dispersing their seeds are extremely ingenious. Plants which produce succulent fruits and berries rely on birds to pick them for eating and to carry them a little way away from the parent plant. Others grow minute downy hairs which catch the wind and lift the tiny seed away to a new site; some others develop little hooks by which they become attached to the fur of animals and so they too get a lift to another, possibly less crowded, area.

The leaves of a plant could very well be termed the 'lungs', since they breathe and absorb through their surfaces what they need from the air and the sunlight. Moisture is mainly taken into the plant by the roots, but when a warm, humid atmosphere envelopes the whole plant, it is especially responded to by the open surfaces of the leaves and this will encourage rapid growth in most cases. Leaves can be found in a wide variety of both size and shape; each type has its own descriptive name and the diagrams show a few of the most common ones. The surface texture of leaves and stems is also of interest to someone trying to identify a wild flower; some, for example, have myriad tiny hairs growing all over them – they are then called downy or hirsute – a disagreeable example of which are the leaves of the common stinging-nettle.

5

a lady's bedstraw

c violet

d mugwort

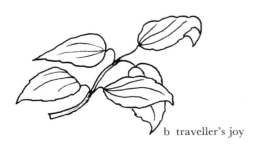

b traveller's joy

6 Leaves from many trees including tamaris, sycamore, beech, willow, apple, may and chestnut; they are mounted on fine white cotton and framed in plain, polished wood.

7

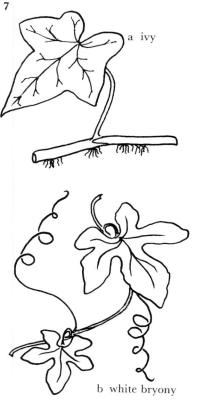

a ivy

b white bryony

The stem of the plant holds the leaves and flowers up to the sunlight in one way or another; in the case of the field buttercup, for example, the stem is robust and erect, while in that of the humble little ivy-leafed toad-flax, the stems creep along sideways and are known as being recumbent. Whatever the style of growth the intention of the plant is to use the stem to lift or carry the flowers and leaves to get a clear view of the sun.

Although most plants manage to grow upwards and find enough space where they can absorb the uninterrupted rays of the sun, one particular group, the climbing plants, have devised different methods of overcoming the grossly over-crowded conditions which exist – to use that sadly over-worked expression correctly for once – at grass-roots level. Some of these vigorous climbers pull themselves up by twisting their small leaf stems around a strong neighbour, as does the traveller's joy, or by winding their main stems round anything adjacent to them, as the bindweed does so successfully. The ivy clings with its tiny rootlets to tree trunks and to walls in its efforts to climb out into clear air, and the white bryony depends on its tendrils to hold itself aloft.

8

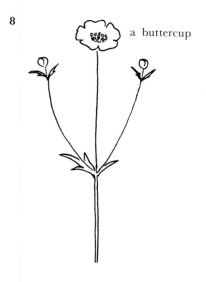

a buttercup

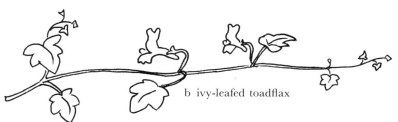

b ivy-leafed toadflax

13

The one part of the plant which we seldom see are the roots, but they, burrowing into the dark soil, absorb both moisture and food which is drawn up into the stem and eventually the cells. Roots adapt themselves to the type of terrain in which they are, and often have to grow deep down in the search for water; they also have an important role in holding the plant steady against strong winds. A number of early spring flowers, like the snowdrop and bluebell, make small bulbs or tubers which are used by the plants to store food against the inhospitable winter months that precede the early flowering.

The selection of flowers for pressing spans ten months of the year and, except for the dark months of November and December when there is very little stirring in the countryside, you will be able to go out along the hedges or into the woods, find a few of them and start your collection. But the first thing which you will need is some help in discovering them.

Discovery means to find and to find out about something, and although nothing could be easier than a walk in the fields where you casually find the wild flowers as you go along, for the complete beginner, the finding out – the identification – can be more difficult and it is helpful to be given some simple well-defined clues. The most obvious thing about the small flower which you have decided to look for will be its *colour*, closely followed by its shape and size. The *overall height* of the plant and the *leaf shape* come next and possibly the type of seed capsule; the *time of the year* when you find it and its *location* are important in confirming your first guess as to its name. These five main points should enable you to identify easily the common wild flowers which have been chosen for pressing. Each one of them is described in careful detail and illustrated with diagrams throughout the book. It should be remembered that plant sizes can vary according to local soil, and that many plants can, in good weather, continue to flower long past their proper season.

The first step to take is to consult the flowering calendar on p. 15; this will show you which of the plants you can expect to be in flower at any time of the year. The chart is arranged alphabetically, starting with bird's foot trefoil and ending with yarrow. You can see that the daisy, for example, holds with the thrift the longest flowering period; if it is the month of May and you want to go out into the countryside for a walk or a picnic and find flowers for your press, then you can look down the column of that month and see at a glance that there are 14 flowers to choose from. After this initial consultation – and you must keep in mind that plants in the north of the country may well be a month or so behind their relations in Sussex or Cornwall – you can look them up individually and discover more about them and where they grow. The relevant page numbers for each plant are given and there you will find clear, basic information about each one, including the five points of identification – illustrated where practicable with small, stylised drawings.

9

To help you recognise the lesser celandine, for example, the notes will show a star-shaped flower face, bright yellow in colour and one which probably measures 3 to 4cm (1–1½in) across. The plant may grow up to 20cm (8in) in height, and notes will tell of any unusual growth pattern. The leaf shape and seed cluster will be outlined too, as

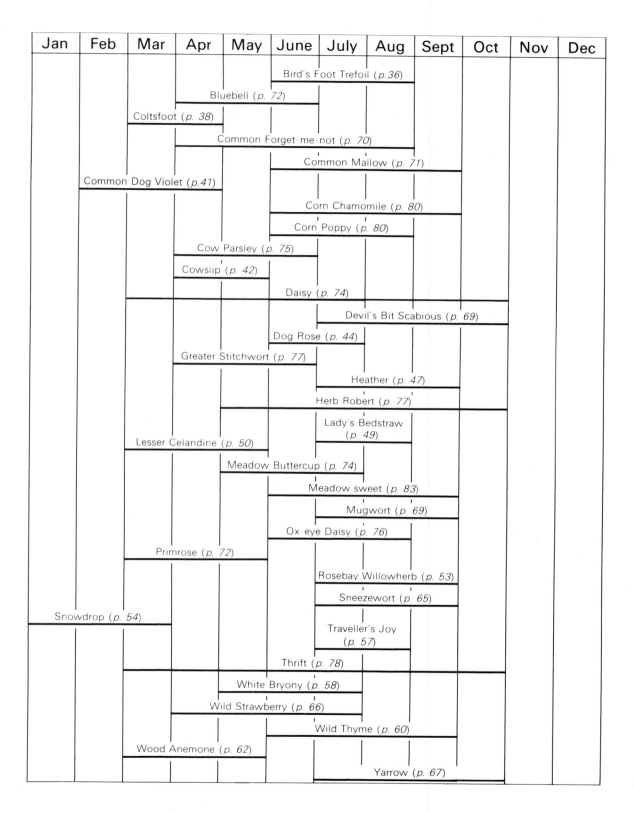

Jan	Feb	Mar	Apr	May	June	July	Aug	Sept	Oct	Nov	Dec

Bird's Foot Trefoil (*p.36*)

Bluebell (*p. 72*)

Coltsfoot (*p. 38*)

Common Forget-me-not (*p. 70*)

Common Mallow (*p. 71*)

Common Dog Violet (*p.41*)

Corn Chamomile (*p. 80*)

Corn Poppy (*p. 80*)

Cow Parsley (*p. 75*)

Cowslip (*p. 42*)

Daisy (*p. 74*)

Devil's Bit Scabious (*p. 69*)

Dog Rose (*p. 44*)

Greater Stitchwort (*p. 77*)

Heather (*p. 47*)

Herb Robert (*p. 77*)

Lady's Bedstraw (*p. 49*)

Lesser Celandine (*p. 50*)

Meadow Buttercup (*p. 74*)

Meadow sweet (*p. 83*)

Mugwort (*p. 69*)

Ox-eye Daisy (*p. 76*)

Primrose (*p. 72*)

Rosebay Willowherb (*p. 53*)

Sneezewort (*p. 65*)

Snowdrop (*p. 54*)

Traveller's Joy (*p. 57*)

Thrift (*p. 78*)

White Bryony (*p. 58*)

Wild Strawberry (*p. 66*)

Wild Thyme (*p. 60*)

Wood Anemone (*p. 62*)

Yarrow (*p. 67*)

this will help in recognition. The note 'March to May' will tell you that in those months the celandine will be in flower, and the last point of information will be that you are most likely to find it in woods and hedgerows and shady places. All this will make the task of finding it very much easier. When you have decided which flower you are going to look for, you can either go into the country taking your book with you, find and identify the plant, cut the necessary flowers, buds and leaves carefully with a pair of scissors or small secateurs and bring it all home to the presss, or you can read up the notes carefully, study the picture and then set out confident that you will recognise your quarry when you find it. Whichever way you do your flower collecting – and it is purely a personal choice – remember to cut down the time between picking and pressing to a minimum. Hot weather and a tight clasp are damaging to delicate wild flowers and you will find that a plastic container with a lid or even a thin plastic bag will cause least harm to them on your journey home.

There is a wide variety of size in the flowers selected for pressing. The violet, for example, is only a modest size: the flowers are seldom more than 1.5cm ($\frac{1}{2}$in) across and the whole plant is small; leaves, flowers, stems and all will fit easily onto a half-page of this book. In contrast, the meadow-sweet towers up 1m (39in) or even more in height and can therefore provide only a small proportion of its flowering spike and the smallest leaves for pressing and a place in one of the designs. Pressed flowers, unless they are artificially trimmed with scissors, must be life-size; they cannot be reduced.

Climbing plants like traveller's joy and white bryony, which by nature rampage all over the hedges, also have to be curtailed by selecting parts of them to fit the limits of the picture. A few flowers and small leaves, some buds and the graceful bend of a stem will recall rather than repeat the habit of the growing plant. Commonsense, in fact, suggests which part of these plants should be pressed, and an artistic feeling for an attractive flower design selects the material to use.

Wild flowers are often so beautiful that it can be difficult to resist the temptation to pick far more than you need. But remember that over the years people have sometimes over-picked the less robust ones which have then become very rare indeed – especially when modern farming methods have widely included the use of selective, so-called 'weed-killers'. Our generation should always try to preserve for the future what we find growing naturally in the countryside.

10 A garland of small wild flowers which include ivy-leafed toadflax, sheep's bit scabious, spring squill, tamaris and willow flowers as well as many others mentioned in this book

2 Picking and Pressing the Wild Flowers

PICKING

Every time you leave the bricks and mortar of the town and go out into the country you will find a few wild flowers. At almost any time of the year some small bloom will catch your eye, and from spring to autumn you will be able to return home from a walk or a picnic with a bunch of wild flowers in your hand. Enjoyable though it may be to find wild flowers like this, it is as well to plan your picking in advance and not to search for them in too haphazard a fashion. If you intend to make a real collection of wild flowers and to be guided by this book, then you will find that, during a twelve-month cycle of natural flowering, you will have more success with pressing if you plan first what you are going to hunt for, reconnoitre to find and identify the best plants and finally go out again to pick. You will know by then exactly what you want and where you will find it, and this knowledge will help eliminate failures in pressing and guard against wasting specimens. Reconnaissance is seldom wasted it is said and this is certainly true when you are picking wild flowers with the serious intention of building up a good collection.

The schedule on p. 15 shows the flowering times of many of the plants used in this book, and from it you can see exactly which ones will be in bloom at any time. At the beginning of a month consult this calendar and familiarise yourself with those plants which will be in flower. Follow up the page references and read the short botanical notes about them and, if you find that these things interest you, then there is further information in Chapter 7 and the glossary (p. 105) about the plant families they belong to and what special features of growth they may have. All the flowers highlighted in this book are commonly found around the British Isles; a very few prefer the north and seldom appear south of that mythical line which crosses the country and finishes in the Wash. There are some which are fussy about their diet and will only grow when their roots are tucked into a good supply of chalk, and there are one or two which relish clinging to cliff tops and mountains; but most of them are widespread and easy to find.

It is essential, when you are picking any of them for your press, that they should be perfect. Try to judge when conditions are right before you pick. Take your time – you may have to keep your eye on a particular patch of ox-eye daisies, or on a shady corner of a wood for the bluebells to open, for some weeks so that you will be able to go and pick them when they are at their best.

There are a few important basic rules which you should remember before you pick anything.

Never pick old material.
Never pick damp material.
Never pick damaged material.
Never pick a single specimen growing by itself.
Never pick more than you need.
Never pick a flower which you have never seen before without finding it first in your wild flower book – it may be rare.
Avoid any plant which appears to have eggs or grubs on it – hatching can take weeks or even months and a tight press or a dry scrapbook will not deter a newly hatched and hungry bug. They, too, like pressed flowers.

Pick your material for pressing on a dry day; even on a fine summer morning wait for the dew to dry. Damp flowers and leaves put straight into the press will grow mould and become unusable in a very short time. Use a sharp pair of secateurs or scissors to cut with and make sure that you do this carefully without damaging the plant. Notice how the plant grows before you choose which flower to cut; observe how the stem stands up from the ground and how the leaves grow in relation to it, and, above all, notice the angle at which the flower hangs on the stalk. Does it face the sun and sky or does it gaze modestly at the ground? When you make up the decorative pictures in this book it will be important to get these natural attitudes right. Again, before you actually cut the flowers for pressing, take note of the size of the flower heads used in the relevant picture; your instinct may well encourage you to press the largest flower head on the plant, but the design which you are going to follow may well require small flowers and modest leaves. It may help you to take the book with you on your country walk so that you can compare size for size.

When you cut for pressing, take one flower on its stem and a single leaf from one plant, and another flowering stem and perhaps a bud from a second. Never strip just a single plant. You will know from the picture how many flowers you are going to need, but it is sensible to pick a few extra ones to allow for failures in the press. In the design for wood anemones (*Figure 66*), for example, you will need eight flowers and 23 leaves as well as the small buds. The accompanying notes on pressing for that flower tell you that the petals may turn brown in the press, and it would be wise, therefore, to take some extra flower heads. These delicate flowers only bloom once a year, and 12 months could be a long time to wait for one extra anemone in order to complete your design!

PRESSING

Always get your fresh material into a press as soon as possible after picking. It is useful to have a small travelling press which you can carry on your walk; clutching fingers will bruise petals and, once flowers have wilted on a hot day, it is difficult to persuade them to recover. In order to press enough wild flowers for the designs in this book you will need a medium-sized flower press, and there is advice on choosing the best type for your needs and where to buy one on p. 26. You should find in

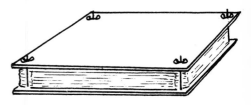

11 Flower press

19

your new press many sheets of blotting paper and similar sized interleaves of card, all cut to fit it exactly and ready to receive your fresh flowers.

Before you actually place the flower material in the press, you must compare it closely with its counterpart in the flower design you are going to copy and read the special pressing notes for that plant. The first step will be to match up the length of your flower on its stem with the picture and, if necessary, cut the bottom of the stem and reduce it roughly to the correct length. Then take the piece in your hand, turn the end of the stem away from you and look down on the top and take a bird's-eye view. Bearing in mind that it is only possible to press successfully in a two-dimensional way, you will now, with your aerial view, be able to decide which leaves and buds and even flowers need to be cut away and pressed separately so that you can press the main spray flat and avoid any unnatural folding of petals or leaf edges. One only has to imagine a thick, luxuriant, flowering spike of rosebay willowherb laid untrimmed on the blotting paper, flattened and crushed in the press for weeks, and emerging as a pink and shapeless blob, to appreciate the necessity of judicious trimming. You will get very much better results if you follow the advice given in the individual pressing notes. Then, when you lift your successfully pressed piece of flowering stem from the press in four to eight weeks' time, you will have material which will enable you to achieve a clear, purely two-dimensional effect. You will be able to add further, separately pressed, leaves, buds and flowers to give a completely natural appearance to the design.

Once the trimming has been completed, open the press and lift off all the top layers of blotting paper and start arranging your flowers on the bottom sheet. Remember at this point to make a note on the corner of the page detailing the name of the plant and the date it was picked. Lay the flowers and leaves, buds and tendrils carefully on the blotting paper, making sure that they lie flat and do not overlap each other. The outline of each piece should be complete and unspoiled as far as possible, foldings and faults in the petals should be avoided at all costs and it is seldom worth putting an old or damaged flower into press. You will see from Figure 12 that you can save space by laying a lot of the flowers head to tail. Try to place flowers of one thickness on a single page of blotting paper – if you mix thick, bulky flower heads with delicate ones there is always a danger that the latter will not be pressed tightly enough. Large flowers and leaves need more space to themselves – lay them sparsely on the page. Some thick buds and seed-heads will need bisecting with a razor blade before they are put into press – not only will they then be much easier to dry but you will double the quantity. Once your flower material is spread carefully on the sheet of blotting paper and there is no more room, cover it gently with another sheet and add more flowers and leaves making a second layer. After every three or four layers of flowers and blotting paper, place an interleaving layer of card or some pages of newspaper cut to size. Last of all put on the top wood board, threading the screws through the holes, put on the nuts and screw down as far as they will go. Put the press in a warm, dry place and next day tighten the nuts still further – you will find there will have been a slight shrinkage already. Continue to

tighten the press every day until it will go no further – hard pressing is essential in preparing perfect flowers. A warm airing cupboard or the corner of the kitchen nearest to the boiler are both excellent places for flower presses.

Check the pages of pressing flowers after ten days to make sure that mould is not forming and that the flowers are pressing well. If any have been inadvertently folded or spoiled you will still have time to collect more specimens and replace them. Leave the flowers and leaves in the press for four to eight weeks, checking occasionally. Drying time depends mostly upon the thickness of the fresh material; some thin, fragile flowers will be ready to use in three or four weeks, but it is safest to err on the side of caution. When the flowers are really dry they will be very light and brittle – some of them almost transparent. Lift them very carefully from the press using small eye-brow tweezers and store them in a folded sheet of blotting paper, a shallow box with a lid, or a plastic file. Make sure that you write the name of the flower and when and where you found it on the outside. Keep them dust free and out of the direct sunlight. Although it can take time to get used to handling the flowers with tweezers, do persevere because you will damage the fragile petals if you handle them with your fingers, however careful you are.

It is always useful to have a supply of clean white blotting paper handy, since you will certainly need some to cut extra sheets for the press as well as for keeping dried flowers in. You will be able to buy blotting paper at most stationers; it is made in standard size of 88 × 58cm (34 × 22in) and you can buy it one sheet at a time or, if you wish to take advantage of wholesale prices, then visit a large shop or one

12 The open flower press showing a page of buttercups. Notice the flowers pressed separately and also the buds and small leaves.

that specialises in office equipment and there you should be able to buy it in packs of 24 sheets at a time – a quire. It will be cheaper this way and if you plan to do a lot of pressing then a big pack will be best in the long run.

Colour changes in flowers during pressing

Some of the flowers and leaves used in this book may change their colour while they are in the press. A few alter quite dramatically, the yellow flowers and small green leaves of lady's bedstraw, for example, will usually turn dark brown or even black when they are dry, and many blue flowers are susceptible to colour loss with the petals turning to a neutral fawn. The pale pink of the fully opened dog rose invariably turns to a deep cream as it dries. From an artistic point of view it is useful to know what to expect in changes of shade and the following list shows some possible colour changes.

buttercup	old flowers turn white
celandine	old flowers may turn white
cowslip	flowers may fade to fawn or turn a little green
cow-wheat	turns very dark brown or black
forget-me-not	old flowers turn to fawn, leaves also
honeysuckle	late flowers tend to dry dark cream or brown
lady's bedstraw	flowers, buds and leaves may turn dark green or black
meadow sweet	buds sometimes darken – beware of mould forming
poppy	poppy-red tends to darken a little to a purple-red
sneezewort	flowers acquire a greyish tinge
snowdrop	petals often deepen to cream
traveller's joy	leaves will darken – almost to brown sometimes
wild rose	opened flowers turn to a deep cream – buds retain the pink
wood anemone	flowers sometimes change to cream

You will see small sprays of grasses, sorrels, ferns and tiny seed-heads used in some of the designs. Always pick these specimens for pressing when they are young, or, in the case of seed-heads, as soon as they have formed. Old grasses and sorrel heads will drop their little flowers very easily after they have been pressed and very old ferns tend to dry a dull, brownish green. Remember to collect pieces of the right size.

Collars

When pressing a thick, 'daisy' type flower, a collar of blotting paper may help to keep the petals flat. Cut out a circle of blotting paper a little larger than the flower, cut a small hole in the centre and push the short flower stem at the back of the petals into it. Place flower and surrounding collar into the press.

Mounts

The petals of some flowers dry semi-transparent and require a backing before they can be successfully used. Cut a piece of tissue paper or thin white paper a little larger than the flower, placing a little adhesive centrally, and press the flower onto it. When the adhesive is dry, cut back the paper to the edges of the petals thus making a 'petticoat' which will deepen the colour.

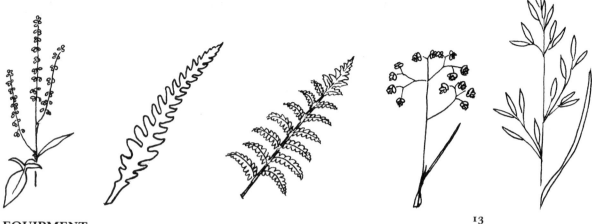

13

EQUIPMENT

The equipment needed for pressing flowers and making the designs is both inexpensive and easy to obtain. What you will need has been listed alphabetically and advice given as to which sort to buy and where to buy it. You will probably find that you already possess a fair proportion of these everyday things and that you actually have to buy very little. For example, the paper clips and Copydex (or similar clear drying adhesive), the small amount of tracing paper and a pair of small eye-brow tweezers are common enough in most households. The costs have not been itemised because there is always some variation between one shop and another and also because prices tend to fluctuate from year to year. The most expensive item which you will have to buy will be the flower press; there is a list on p. 118 of various stockists which may be helpful to you if you live in the country and are far from the large department stores. But, however you set about equipping yourself for this new hobby, you will find that the outlay in financial terms is not high and that you will have little difficulty in obtaining what you need.

Where to keep your flowers once they are pressed, together with all the small tools of your trade, is worth considering. Dust and strong sunlight, a sudden draught of wind as well as prying fingers are all your enemies, and it is advisable to put everything away safely in a cupboard or a special drawer every time you finish using them. Alternatively they can be kept on a large tray or a two-tiered tea-trolley covered over with a dark coloured cloth.

Adhesive – Copydex
This well-known white adhesive dries almost clear and it is excellent for sticking down pressed flowers. Be careful not to spill it on to fabric – it may leave a shiny mark. A little goes a long way with this adhesive and a tube will last a very long time. There are other similar types on the market which will serve your purpose equally well.

Album

The modern type of photograph album has self-adhesive pages each covered with a thin plastic skin which can be peeled back and easily replaced. An album of this sort can be used very satisfactorily for holding your flower pictures. They can be closely inspected and admired but not touched. The pages of these albums are usually punched with two holes and can be detached from the spine while you work on them and ultimately replaced. Both sides of the page can be used. The small sized album, 23cm (9in) square, will probably be the best size for wild flowers.

The traditional scrap-book or a stick-in photograph album with plain card pages are excellent for mounting the flowers and will in many ways give a more pleasing final effect than the modern ones, since there will be no artificial shiny layer between your regard and the flowers themselves. Buy them at a reputable stationers and look for quality. Choose pages of a colour that will flatter your small flower designs and not overpower them (*see Fig. 14*). Large department stores will often stock these albums.

Backgrounds
See Card and Fabrics

Biros and pens
Keep an assortment in your equipment box ranging from the extra fine to the thicker, fibre-tipped types. You will need them for recording the names of your flowers, noting when and where you found them, as well as for drawing ornamental borders round your designs if you have a steady hand and a liking for such things.

Blotting paper
Standard quality blotting paper can be bought from most stationers. White is perhaps the best, but any colour will do. Wholesale or office stationers will sell by the quire, which is the minimum wholesale quantity, comprising 24 sheets each measuring 88 × 58cm (34 × 22in); this will be the cheapest way to buy it. Remember that you will need a lot of blotting paper if you press a lot of flowers and leaves.

Books
See Wild flower books

Card
You can get card from stationers and art shops. It is made in many colours, qualities and thicknesses. Soft, pale shades such as grey, off-white, cream and buff will probably make the best backgrounds for your flowers to start with.

Fabrics
You will need fine material for using as a base for some of your flower designs and, because it will be laid over the printed outline design on the page, it must be semi-transparent. Cotton organdie is perfect for this as it has a natural stiffness which makes it easy to handle, but you will find others such as fine lawns and muslin equally good provided they are well clipped down and drawn tightly across the page. Search for them in the material departments of large stores as well as in small local fabric shops. Since you will only need a very small yardage for each picture, remember to look in the pile of remnants.

Vilene is excellent; it is a man-made fibre used by dressmakers as a lining material for stiffening. It can be bought in both white and cream and in several different weights or thicknesses. The type you choose for your flower picture base is a matter of personal preference, but the medium weight will probably be both easiest to handle and the best. Ask for the non-iron-on type.

Fabrics which can be used for backgrounds when following methods 2 and 3 include silks, cottons, dupions, good-quality polyesters and lining materials. Velvet and very shiny satins and fabrics with a loose weave are all difficult to manage. Although soft shades of green, grey and cream are excellent, keep a few pieces in a brighter shade. Black and scarlet can be very effective. (See also Lining.)

Frames

Small, ready-made frames with the glass and backing suitable for framing your relatively small flower designs can be bought from large stores and also from photograph shops. In frame shops you should be able to buy ready-made, oval or circular ones and also have rectangular ones made up to your requirements. Look in antique shops, sale rooms or jumble sales for small, old frames; well cleaned and polished and with a little repair work done, they can be used for your wild flowers most successfully.

Gums and glues

Keep some in your box – one for sticking paper to paper and a stronger one for gluing wood surfaces in case of small frame repairs. A tube of Copydex or similar latex-based adhesive will be needed for making your pictures.

Lining (iron-on)

Sold commonly under the brand name Vilene, it can be ironed on to the back of a piece of fabric to give it 'body' before the flowers are stuck down. Enquire at haberdashery departments and fabrics shops.

Masking tape

Less powerful than the usual Sellotape, and ideal for fixing a design on to a mount. It is usually pale cream in colour and is sold by the roll at stationers and hardware stores. A width of 1.2cm ($\frac{1}{2}$in) or 2cm ($\frac{3}{4}$in) will be sufficient for your purpose.

Mounts

A mount is a piece of paper-surfaced card cut the same size as the internal measurements of a picture frame, with the whole of the centre cut out very neatly in any shape that you choose: round, oval or rectangular. Your pressed flowers will be placed in the centre of it so that the coloured card surrounding them will make a complementary border. You can obtain a mount from picture framers – take your frame with you to the shop as well as the measurements of your flower design and the framer will cut a mount specially for you. The cost will not be excessive but you should enquire first.

Paper

In choosing a suitable paper on which to mount your flowers, remember that it must have the necessary transparency so that the black outlined flower picture on the page beneath can show through. Tracing paper, thin copy paper and airmail writing paper (the unusual 'seersucker' surface type is very good), all have this factor and can easily be bought and used as bases. The rice paper which is used in cooking to back macaroons is excellent; it has one surface which, although shiny, has a dimpled effect and this makes a very attractive background for flowers. Tissue paper, too, which has the advantage of being available in a beautiful wide range of colours, will also serve your purpose well. For mounting your own wild flower designs, there is a wide range of papers available from art shops and large stationers. This type of art paper is sold in large sheets.

Paper clips

Strong clips, such as bulldogs or a similar variety, will be needed when you are making a design. You will have to clip them around the page that you are working on – holding the base to the page. Three or four will be necessary and about 2.5cm (1in) to 4cm (1½in) wide will be large enough.

If you decide to store your dried flower material in between blotting paper folders, it is advisable to fasten the edges together since they have an unhappy habit of sliding out. Ordinary paper clips are perfectly adequate in this case.

Pencils

Keep an assortment in your box and a soft india-rubber. Hard pencils are marked H and soft ones that make a heavy black line are known as B. An HB is the type generally used for writing.

Press

A flower press can be obtained from either a large general store which has an art and craft department or from a craft shop. Make sure that the corner screws and butterfly nuts are of good quality and screw down freely, and also that the wood base and top are sound. You will be putting a considerable pressure on them when it is full of your flowers laid between the layers of blotting paper. A useful size for wild flowers will be about 28cm (11in) square. (The very small flower presses are really only useful as a temporary measure when you are out for the day or on holiday and want one which will slip easily into the picnic basket or a large pocket.) It is also satisfactory to use an old fashioned trouser press or even a tie press; they can be found in junk shops and at jumble sales and will not cost much. A word of warning: they can be very heavy and the large screws can be a little hazardous when you carry them around the house.

Ruler

Keep one in your box – preferably the clear plastic type – for straight lines and general measuring.

Scissors

You will need a large pair for cutting flowers, paper and material and a small pair for trimming flowers before you put them into press and later while you are making the designs. Both need to be sharp, the points meeting accurately.

Storage files

Clear, stiff plastic office files are inexpensive and useful for storing your pressed flowers and leaves. They will keep everything safely flat and you can see at a glance what material you have available – although you must remember to put them away in the dark after use. Shallow cardboard boxes with lids can also be used satisfactorily, as can simple blotting paper folders held together with paper clips. A small cabinet with shallow drawers of the type used by dentists is probably the best of all, but these are very difficult to obtain.

Tracing paper

The best for your use will be tracing paper which is sold in flat packs – standard quality and the A4 size (210×297mm [$8\frac{1}{4} \times 11\frac{3}{5}$in]) – at stationers. Rolls of paper are very awkward indeed to persuade to lie flat unless they are pinned down.

Tweezers

The small eye-brow or stamp collector's variety are essential for your delicate work. The former type are perfectly adequate and can be bought from chemists. Make sure that the ends are not rough and that they meet properly.

Wild flower books

There are many books on the subject available on the market and they range from the most basic, which supply the merest minimum of botanical information and are often illustrated by poor-coloured and inaccurate pictures, to those which are so immensely informative that it is difficult to find what you are looking for. Somewhere in the middle of the two extremes there are excellent books using a straightforward approach and modern language, the pages made attractive with fine coloured drawings or photographs. Those listed in the bibliography (p. 118) are some of the well-tried favourites.

3 Making the Flower Designs

By the time you read and study this chapter you will have some wild flowers pressed and ready for use and be impatient to make up a design and enjoy the aesthetic pleasure which can be found in its creation.

Before you actually begin on the work, however, you should read through the instructions and advice in this chapter and then ask yourself two questions. Which method of construction would be best for me to follow with these flowers? What am I going to do with the design of flowers once it is finished? Pressed flowers are very fragile and cannot be left unprotected for long.

Once you have the two answers in your mind then you will know on which type of background material to mount your flowers and which method of construction to choose; you will then be able to gather together the materials and equipment you are going to need. You should also decide where you are going to work. Remember that this is a time-consuming, peaceful hobby and one that may well occupy you for several hours. Choose a place where you can put out all your things and where they can be left undisturbed if you have to break off your work and return to it later. Jolts, a gust of air, small enquiring fingers or the family cat can wreak havoc once you have begun. Work, therefore, on a firm table in a well-lit position, with enough space for all your things, away from open windows and doors, and have available some protective sheets of card or thick paper which can be placed on top of everything to safeguard it, if necessary.

There are three basic methods set out in this chapter which can be followed when you are making a design with pressed flowers. The first two can only be used when there is a pattern drawing provided, as in Chapter 4 and sometimes in Chapter 5; method 3, however, must be followed for all the other designs in the book which have no accompanying life-size drawing.

Although using method 1 will be found especially satisfactory for those of you with limited experience, it should be pointed out that method 3 can be used perfectly well for making all the flower illustrations. When you become very proficient in handling the flowers, you may find that you enjoy creating every picture in this way.

The basic equipment needed for all three methods is simple and consists of a tube of a latex-based adhesive (Copydex is ideal), small

eye-brow tweezers, an ash-tray or similar sized flat dish, a wooden cocktail stick or a well-sharpened matchstick, a few sewing pins and a pair of sharp nail-scissors, three or four bulldog or similar clips and your store of flowers and leaves. When you are following methods 1 and 2 you will also require a piece of semi-transparent material large enough to fit over the pattern drawing and to reach at least two edges of the page. Suggestions for suitable material are made under the headings 'Fabrics' (p. 24) and 'Paper' (p. 25.) Which base material to have is a matter of personal choice, but it is easier to work on a type which has a firm body to it. Soft muslin, for example, would be difficult to hold in position when you are attaching the flowers, whilst tissue paper would increase the likelihood of damage once the design was completed. Tracing or rice paper, white Vilene or organdie are all excellent.

If you are following method 3, then you will stick your flowers direct onto a non-transparent background and your task will be made easier if you work on one with some body to it. Stiff paper, card and most fabrics backed with iron-on Vilene are excellent. Always prepare a piece larger than the frame, calendar or mount. You can cut it down to size after you have finished the delicate work.

METHOD 1

Following this scheme you are going to construct your flower picture on a semi-transparent base material laid over the pattern drawing. The lines of the pattern will show you exactly where to place your pressed material and the stylised, numbered accompanying drawing will tell you the order in which the flowers and leaves should be laid down.

Start with number 1 and work through in ascending order of numbers, finally adding small pieces of grass or stem, perhaps, as trimmings to complete it to your artistic satisfaction.

Read these instructions carefully before you start and inspect both the pattern drawing and the numbered one so that you fully understand how you are going to work through the diagram.

14 Part of a work table set by a window. The stage-by-stage construction of a flower design can be seen and the album holds the completed picture of cowslips.

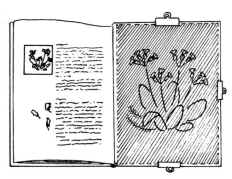

15 A transparent base fixed over the pattern drawing of cowslips. The three clips hold it firmly in place and the numbered drawing is opposite.

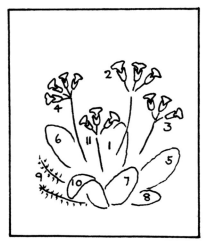

16 A stylised drawing of the cowslip design, numbered to show the order in which the material is added.

1 Open the book at the place where the drawing is and make sure that the page is as flat as possible. Measure the width of the page, then a sufficient length down to cover the pattern comfortably, and cut a rectangle of base material to that size. Ensure that you cut along the drawing will show through (*see Figure 15*).

2 Clip the base on to the page with two or three large clips, lining up the threads with the page edges. The strong black lines of the pattern drawing will show through (see Figure 15).

3 Search in your store of appropriate flowers for ones that closely resemble those in the pattern. Sufficient flowers, buds, leaves and stems, etc., should all be placed on a piece of card or paper beside you.

4 Consult the numbered drawing (*Figure 16*) and, starting with number 1, choose a flower which is of similar size and stance and lay it on the base exactly over its twin in the pattern underneath. Trim the length of the stalk with the scissors, if necessary. Do not stick the material down at this point, simply assemble the whole design loose on the base. Match up the centre point of your flower heads exactly with the centre of the flowers in the pattern drawing. Ensure that they tilt the right way and that the leaves are the right side up. It is usually advisable to match the leaf up to the one in the drawing from the outside point inwards to the design centre. You will be able to cover any shortfall of stem or leaf with a small bit of extra material and this will not spoil the overall balance of the design.

5 When you have completed the design thus far, lift off most of the pieces and place them to one side, leaving only numbers 1, 2 and 3 on the base. You are now ready to fix down the flowers. Squeeze a little of the adhesive on to the flat dish and have ready the little stick. Lift number 1 in the tweezers and turn it towards you and touch the back of the stalk in two places with a very small amount of adhesive. It should usually be placed at the bottom and two thirds the way up the length of stem or the leaf. The smaller the amount of adhesive the better. Place the piece of pressed material gently down on to the base exactly covering the twin in the drawing underneath.

6 Follow on in the same manner with numbers 2 and 3, etc., checking each time that *your* rapidly forming design is matching up with the drawing underneath. Once you have begun to stick material down, carry on through all the numbers until it is finished and then immediately unclip the edges, place a piece of firm paper over it and lift it off, turning it over and laying it down on the table, reverse side uppermost to dry. (Because of the flimsy nature of some base materials you may find that a little of the adhesive may have soaked through on to

17 Some examples of pressed material showing where to place the small points of adhesive.

the pattern drawing beneath. One of the good qualities of this type of adhesive is that it will wipe or peel off most paper surfaces without leaving a mark.) Your design is now completed, and for further instructions see p. 32.

METHOD 2

You will need to follow this second method if you wish to mount your flower design on to a material which is not transparent. For example, you may think that the little snowdrops in Figure 54 would look very attractive mounted on a dark green silk or cotton, and neither of these fabrics will enable you to see through to the pattern drawing. You will have to work first on a base rectangle of either tracing paper or rice paper and then to remount onto the thicker background. Follow instructions set out in method 1, with the only difference being that in number 5 the two smearings of adhesive must be as close to the *bottom* of the stem as possible and, if necessary, reduced to one. Complete with number 6 and then carry on as follows.

1 Once you have turned the completed flower design upside down, allow plenty of time for the adhesive to dry and for the paper base to become stiff again.

2 Using the nail-scissors, cut away the transparent base material around the centre boss where all the gluing has been done and lift away the surrounding loose paper. Trim back neatly as close to the gluing points as possible so that the remaining paper will not show when the design is the right way up.

For more instructions on how to mount or frame the design see pp. 33–5.

METHOD 3

With this scheme you will be using your own artistic skill to fashion a design with the flowers. The photograph or drawing will provide your imagination with a possible idea and will assist you if you wish to copy it, but a great deal of the re-creation of it will come from you. This time it will not be possible to have a pattern drawing to help you, as many of the flower pictures are either too large or too complicated.

 Prepare a piece of background material of firm paper, card or fabric backed with iron-on Vilene and cut it large enough to accommodate the flowers and foliage and a possible frame as well. You will need to cut it down to size afterwards.

 Using the illustration of the completed picture as a guide, copy it using your own pressed leaves and flowers. The numbered stylised diagram, given where necessary, will show the order in which the pieces should be added. You will find that there is an overall approach of construction with flower design which usually follows what could be termed a 'compass point' system. Points at north, south, east and west should be laid down in that order and the intervening sections then completed if they are due to be filled in. With this basic outline settled you can then follow on with a concentric building inwards to the focal point.

 Where possible lay a chosen frame over the background while you work and arrange the flowers within its measurements. Always leave

a Flower design made by method 2, the dotted circle showing where to cut back.

b Compass point construction.

18

31

sufficient space between the frame edge and the flower design – especially at the top and the bottom.

1 Make a selection of the type of flowers and leaves that you are going to need and lay them on a sheet of paper beside you.

2 Beginning with the topmost point in the picture, choose a spray that is similar in size and shape and lay it down on the background at the point north. (Do not stick anything down now.)

3 Follow on with the pieces which will be at the point south at the bottom of the picture and then move on to the east on the righthand side and then the west on the left.

4 Adjust them to the measurement of any frame or mount that you are working with and ensure that the gap between the main points of outline and the frame edge are correct and balancing.

5 Fill in the intervening points around the outline and adjust the angles of the stems so that there is a flow of 'line' through the picture. You should be beginning to feel the *shape* and artistic flow in the design by now.

6 Begin to fill in the centre, always keeping a balance between each side, working roughly round and round in towards the centre. Do not overcrowd and allow some of the stalks running down behind the design to appear.

7 Choose one or two large blossoms with good colour and perfect shape for the centre or focal point of the design.

8 Now that the design is complete, you must begin to fix it down. Remove all the loose, pressed material carefully from the background and put it to one side leaving the four main compass points *in situ*. Using the adhesive, and working through north, south, east and west, smear each one in turn in two places and return it to its position on the background. (Put the adhesive at the bottom and two-thirds way up the stems on the reverse side.)

9 Continue to replace all pressed material with adhesive until you have re-formed the design to your satisfaction.

COMPLETION AND PROTECTION

As has been suggested at the beginning of this chapter, it is sensible to plan ahead before you start work. You have now read through the three basic methods of construction and must consider what you are going to do with the flower design once it is completed. These designs with their fragile flowers can easily be damaged and it is best to put them in a place of safety or to give them some protection so that they can be looked at and enjoyed in the future.

For an album

Perhaps you are going to make a picture to fit into an album to form part of a collection of wild flowers, in which case it may be best to use a paper base material. If you have been using method 1 you will be able to cut the finished design down neatly to the size of your album page and stick it straight in. Measure the size accurately, mark softly with a pencil and cut cleanly, preferably with a guillotine. Stick down with a

19 Two pages of an album showing snowdrops and notes of where and when they were picked.

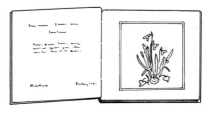

20 A simple picture of grey mugwort leaves mounted on dark green card. The frame is green and silver.

good paper glue and allow to dry. An ink line drawn around the edge either in black, gold or with any fibre-tipped coloured pen can give an attractive final touch. If you have made a free design using method 3 for inclusion in the album, then you can mount it either on semi-transparent paper stretched over any piece of card, or you can work directly on to a rectangle of ordinary good-quality paper or card, sticking it into place once the adhesive is dry.

For a framed picture
If you have decided instead to frame the design and make a traditional picture with it, and have followed method 1, then you will need to back the thin base material with something firmer before you can fix it into a frame. Choose the frame and a fabric background which will complement both frame shade, the transparency of the base material and the flowers. Cut a piece larger than the frame. Have ready the completed design which will be upside down, drying. Place a wide smear of Copydex on to the centre boss and, with great care, turn over and stick it into the centre of the background. White base material such

as Vilene, organdie or any of the papers will look very effective if they are laid over a second white surface, as can be seen in the picture of poppies (colour plate 1).

If you have followed method 2 you will now have a completed design in which the stems of the flowers and leaves are only attached to the central boss by their tips, and all the rest of the base material has been cut away. They require careful mounting on to another coloured background. Cut this out – again with a little yardage to spare all round. The flower design will be upside down and now dry, and you can put a good smear of Copydex on the central boss and place the piece of background fabric on top of it. Cover the two with a piece of firm card and turn them all over. To give extra security to the long, loose flower stems, lift them one by one away from the material with a pin and place a minute smear of adhesive underneath, and allow each one to fall back gently into its correct position. (Check that the main upright line through the flowers runs parallel to the line in the fabric.)

If, however, you have followed method 3 and worked directly on to a fabric, then your task will be simpler and you can frame up your picture without any more ado.

Now you will have a flower design ready for framing whichever method you have employed in the construction.

Framing a picture

Work on a soft surface and keep everything very clean and dust free. Place the frame and the glass beside your design. Lay the clean glass on top of the flowers, check that the edges run along the threads of the fabric and then place the frame over it, checking the placing of the whole flower shape inside. Lift off and then mark around the glass with a pencil. Cut along this line and place the flowers to one side. Using the glass again as a template, cut out a piece of white paper to act as a liner behind the flowers, and then several shapes from thick magazine pages to give bulk. (A layer of thin cotton blanket is often effective here and can produce the attractive padded look.) Finally cut a shape in thick card for the frame backing.

Place the frame face downwards on the table, put the glass into the rebate, followed by the flowers, the white paper and the loose pages or blanket and the card backing (adjust the number of wadding pages to fill the rebate sufficiently).

Using small tacks, a pair of jeweller's tweezers and a tack hammer, fasten down the back. Do not use more tacks than necessary and the heads should be covered with strips of masking tape before you glue on a final overall covering of paper. Fix small screws and rings at the back; attach some fine cord and the picture will be ready for hanging on the wall.

For a mount

You will see in several of the illustrations that flowers have been placed in card mounts. These inexpensive surrounds can set off a simple picture to great effect.

If you want to use a mount it is advisable to take the little flower design along to a framing or art shop and get one cut to a specific shade and size. You should be able to get advice on both these matters but be

21 A mount with a completed flower design fixed in it by short strips of masking tape (reverse side).

careful not to choose a shade of card which overshadows the soft colour of wild flowers. Ask for an estimate of cost, but normally these basic mounts are not very expensive.

To fix a picture in, lay the mount over the flowers and mark the fabric with a pencil along the edges. Cut back the fabric so that it will be 1 cm ($\frac{3}{8}$in) or so smaller than the outside measurement of the mount. Cut four small pieces of masking tape and place each one half-way under an edge of the picture fabric. (The picture should be face upwards on the table and there should now be a small sticky tab protruding out from each side.) Hold the mount carefully over the picture and, when it is in exactly the correct position, lower it firmly and press down. The four tabs will catch hold and, when you turn the whole over on to its face, the picture will not move. Now cut and stick down four longer strips of tape and the picture will be really secure. It is now ready for future framing or for keeping in a collection.

Flower pictures without adhesives
When you are following method 3, it is just as satisfactory to dispense with the adhesive and to lay the flowers loosely on the background, framing them up in such a manner that they are held in place between the glass and frame backing. It is entirely a matter of personal preference whether you stick them down or lay them loose, and when you are making a picture solely for framing up into a picture you will have a choice of these two methods to follow.

Framing loose flowers is not difficult but you must first get your frame complete with glass and stiff card (or hardboard) backing. Cut out your coloured background material using the glass as a template, and then cut a second similar shape of lining in a soft flannelette or thin wadding. Place the card (or hardboard) backing on the table in front of you and put the lining shape on top, followed by the coloured background material. You must work directly on to this, laying the flowers loosely on to the design. (Hold the frame in place occasionally during your work to ensure that the balance between the bulk of the design and the frame edge is pleasing.)

Work through instructions 1–7 for method 3 (p. 32), arranging the flowers until they meet with your artistic approval and then gently lower the glass on top, followed by the frame. The whole must then be picked up, pinched tightly between the fingers and turned over to be laid face down on a soft surface. Fasten the picture down securely with tiny tacks or panel pins, either pushing them in firmly with small jeweller's pliers or knocking them in a little with a small tack hammer. Cover the nail heads with masking tape or backing paper.

4 Wild Flowers in Simple Designs

This chapter shows how 14 of our common wild flowers can be used, once they are pressed, to make attractive pictures which will display not only their charm but their manner of growth. They have been arranged alphabetically and not in their natural sequence of flowering. These are simple pictures and, if you follow the instructions set out in the previous chapter, you should have no difficulty in completing them all.

With each plant you will be able to study a photograph of the design made with the blossoms and leaves and there will be a clear pattern drawing of it to guide you when you are constructing your picture with your own pressed material. There will be short botanical details and some general notes about the plant, its country names and its history. There will be a small diagramatic, numbered drawing which will show the order of assembly and some further notes to augment this operation.

BIRD'S FOOT TREFOIL *Lotus corniculatus*
LEGUMINOSAE FAMILY

Bright yellow pea-shaped flower with large 'keel' – sometimes tinged with red or orange. In flat clusters of three to eight flowers.

Five leaflets, a trefoil at the top and a pair at the base near the stem.

Straight pods with a curved spur at the ends. 15–30mm ($\frac{5}{8}$–$1\frac{1}{4}$in) long. They split and twist to scatter the seed when ripe.

Height: 10–40cm (4–16in).

Habitat: Widespread throughout the British Isles in grassland, road verges and garden lawns.

Flowering: June to September.

This is a common and familiar summer flowering plant. It seems to thrive on most soils and in varying climates so that you will find it tucked in amongst the grass along the sheltered verges of inland roads just as easily as you will high on the cliffs near the sea. The flowers are a bright yellow, but it is quite usual to find them tinged with orange or even red and this mixture of colours gives rise to one of the country names of 'eggs and bacon'.

Bird's foot trefoil is a low-growing plant with short straight stems holding up the pea-shaped flowers in their rather flat clusters. Once the pods begin to form, the flowers shrivel and fall leaving the straight pods pointing outwards around the stalk, reminiscent in shape of a bird's claw, thus giving the plant its most familiar name. The pods split open and twist in order to scatter the seeds. The word 'trefoil', which refers to the foliage, is an inaccurate one, for each leaf has five little leaflets, not three, as suggested.

There are said to be as many as 70 different local names given to this attractive low-growing wild flower, including Tom thumb, Lady's shoes and stockings, God Almighty's thumb and fingers, and Crow toes.

You will see bees and even wasps visiting the flower for the nectar and these rather heavy insects will be able to pollinate the plant.

Pressing notes
These flowers are simple to press despite their clustered heads. Even the new formed pods will dry well in the press. Remember to press those stems which are going to curve in the right way for inclusion in your design.

Small tufts of grass which have been kept low-growing by grazing sheep can be picked to complete this picture.

Assembling the design
This is a simple picture to make as only six pieces are required. Read the instructions on p. 38 very carefully and make sure that you understand them fully. When you have clipped your semi-transparent base over the pattern drawing, collect your pieces of pressed flower and leaf

23 An arrangement of bird's foot trefoil with short grass. The mount is deep blue.

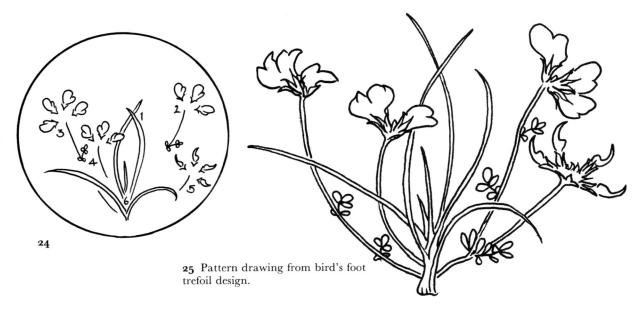

24

25 Pattern drawing from bird's foot trefoil design.

material and place them ready beside you. Following the numbered diagram, first place a gently curving piece of grass centrally, making sure that the top and bottom most points are correctly in line with the pattern beneath. Continue with a curving stem flower head, number 2, then follow with number 3 and make sure that the flower centres lie exactly over the corresponding centres in the pattern. Continue with the next two pieces (numbers 4 and 5) and complete the shape, whilst number 6, a small tuft of grass, builds in the centre. Note that the flower on the right hand side (number 5) is practically over. The florets have shrivelled and the immature pods within already give a good impression of the sharp-clawed foot of a bird.

Once you have completed the design, remove all the material and place it on one side. Re-form the design again over the pattern, this time applying small amounts of adhesive to the top and bottom of each piece before laying them over their shadows underneath.

The small circular picture has been mounted in a dark blue mount (*see Figure 23*) and this confirms the curving nature of the design and accentuates the darkest shade in the bird's foot trefoil.

COLTSFOOT *Tussilago farfara* COMPOSITAE FAMILY

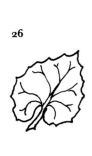

26

Bright yellow – about 3cm (1¼in) in diameter. Composed of both types of florets – a ring of 'ray' florets surrounding a centre knob of 'disc' ones. Sepals and stem scales are purplish-green.

Heart shaped, broad and a strong green with pointed teeth irregularly placed around the edge. Undersides are white, downy. Up to 20cm (8in) in diameter appearing after the flowers have finished blooming.

Clusters of silky down – the seed is spread by wind.

Height: 15–30cm (6–12in).

Habitat: Bare and waste ground throughout the British Isles.

Flowering: March and April.

The coltsfoot in flower is a welcome sight in early spring, the sulphur-yellow flowers brightening poor and neglected ground. The flower stems are knobbly with purplish-green scales which give the plant a slightly bizarre appearance, heightened by the fact that there are no leaves to mask them. The flowers, each about the size of a 50 pence piece, bloom and finish before the leaves appear and it may be this unusual order of growth which gave rise to the old country name of 'son before father'. The usual name of coltsfoot is probably derived from the shape of the leaf, reminiscent of a hoof mark and often as large. They will grow up to 20cm (8in) across and the undersides are woolly with a white, felt-like covering which was scraped off and used as tinder in days gone by.

After flowering, the seed-heads become fat and fluffy with dozens of small silvery 'parachutes', each attached to a seed, and eventually they are caught by the wind and carried away from the parent plant. Goldfinches often use this soft down to line their nests and can be seen flying along with a large puff-ball of it in their beaks.

Coltsfoot was in great demand in olden days to alleviate coughs and chest troubles; a syrup made from the leaves was prescribed for a 'hot, dry cough, wheezing and shortness of breath', while smoking the dried and rolled leaves was deemed a help for asthma sufferers.

Gardeners are not fond of coltsfoot and, understandably, it is considered by them to be a troublesome weed, strongly rooting and seeding itself everywhere.

Two curling pieces of ivy have been used to finish off the bottom of

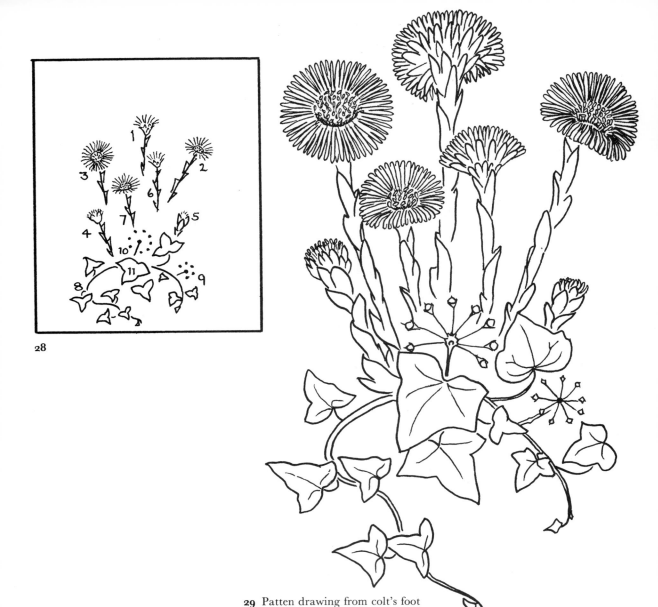

29 Patten drawing from colt's foot design.

the flower design. This robust, climbing plant can be found in woods and on waste ground at any time of the year, growing over neglected banks and on tree trunks. In the winter time the black seeds are a favourite food for hungry birds.

Pressing notes
When picking coltsfoot you may have to take the press to the plant; the flowers must go into the press quickly before they close up. If this does occur, then stand them in a little water in a sunny window and they will probably re-open. When pressing the larger, fully open flowers, cut them off the stems, press the two parts separately and re-assemble after drying. Smaller flowers can be bent over firmly on to blotting paper with the thumb, or simply pressed in profile. The small un-opened buds

are very thick and they will require a little extra space to themselves on the page. Coltsfoot presses well but, once dry, the sharp yellow can fade if left in strong sunlight. Ivy also presses well, but when you put a small trail into press try not to allow the smaller leaves to lie across the hard stems – detach them and lay them on the blotting paper by themselves. Choose small seed-heads and put them direct into press – surprisingly there is no need to trim away any of the individual seeds since they will obligingly splay out like the face of a clock, once the pressure is exerted.

Assembling the design

Although in the diagram (*Figure 28*) the bottoms of the flower stems have been omitted for the sake of clarity, when you are placing the flower material on to the base, allow the stems to run down behind the ivy seed-head to the imaginary ground, and trim them to that length.

COMMON VIOLET *Viola riviniana* VIOLACEAE FAMILY

Typical violet shape, 15–25mm ($\frac{5}{8}$–1in) across, blue-purple in colour the spur pale and indented at the tip and the sepals pointed. Scentless.

Cordate and pointed at the tip with gently indented edges.

Seed capsule breaks open into three segments.

Height: Up to 20cm (8in).

Habitat: Very common throughout the British Isles. Hedges, banks and the edges of woods, also on mountains.

Flowering: March to June.

For many people violets will fall simply into one of two categories, they are either scented or they are not, and *Viola riviniana* belongs to the latter group. Despite its lack of sweet smell it is a beautiful little purple flower and grows freely all through the British Isles. During the months of April, May and June a walk through any sheltered part of the countryside will probably find you some of these much-loved wild flowers. They are low-growing and fairly compact, as Figure 31 shows, although later in their flowering season they can acquire a straggly appearance with the flowers branching off ever-lengthening side shoots.

31 A circular group of violets put into a cream coloured mount.

The flowers, with their well-known distinctive shape, are a true violet in shade and the spur at the back of the flower is pale with a slight indentation at the tip. The leaves are heart-shaped – *cordate* to give the botanical term – and the edges are gently notched.

In a floral dictionary of 1854, where different qualities and attributes were allocated to different flowers, the violet meant 'modesty' – a happy choice for a lady's buttonhole.

Violet petals have been sugared and dried by cooks for many years. In Turkey they are reputed to have been used to make the most famous and delicious of sorbets 100 years ago, and today we use crystallised violets to decorate our cakes and fine chocolates.

The seed-capsule is triangular and shaped at first like a small pointed egg. When the seeds inside are swollen and ripe it splits open three ways. Despite its delicate appearance it is a strongly growing small plant and, given all but the most adverse conditions, will set up a colony in a short space of time.

Pressing notes
Violet flowers are difficult to press because of their shape. Try to press some full-face as well as in profile. For the former, trim away the stalk and possibly a little of the spur at the back of the flower before laying it firmly down on to the blotting paper. When pressing in profile, make sure that the petals are laid correctly and again encourage the flower head to remain flat with gentle pressure of a thumb. Pick and press flowers which have just opened – the blue is a fugitive shade and flowers tend to fade while drying. Always press a few extra to allow for failure.

The leaves, however, will press excellently, as will the side-shoots complete with un-opened buds. The material will dry in a few weeks in the press – treat it carefully, it will be very fragile.

33 Pattern drawing from common violet design.

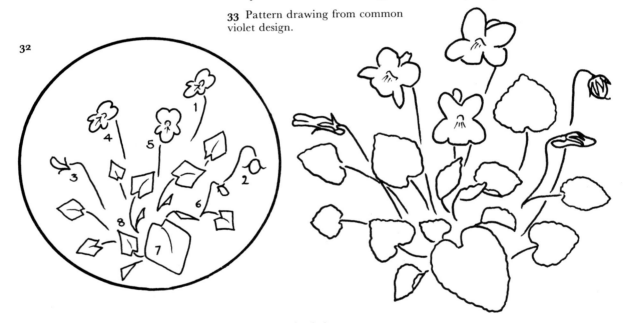

32

Assembling the design
This design is quite straightforward to make and there is no need to use any other plant material – the compact shape of the small plant fills in a circular mount extremely well.

Start with number 1 on the chart and work carefully through to completion – but always keep the picture out of strong sunlight as the blue will continue to fade.

COWSLIP *Primula veris* **PRIMULACEAE FAMILY** (see p. 29)

Deep yellow with orange spot in the centre, the five petals (each slightly notched) are joined together within the green sepals to form a tube.

Clustered in groups of up to 30 flowers, hanging one-sided on the stem. 10–15mm ($\frac{3}{8}$–$\frac{5}{8}$in) in size and with a sweet fragrance.

Ovate and fairly large, wrinkled and downy on both sides, pale green in shade. Abruptly narrowing as they approach the base.

A long capsule which has five teeth at the top.

Height: 10–30cm (4–12in).

Habitat: Grasslands and meadows on chalk, limestone and clay in England, Wales and central Ireland.

Flowering: April to May.

Cowslips have taken heavy punishment over the years from people picking their fragrant flowers to make cowslip wine. You need a lot of blossoms to make six bottles – about half a pillowcase-full according to Mrs Beeton's recipe – and so the population of this lovely plant has declined in these islands, and we are the losers.

Fortunately there are still cowslips growing on the grassy downlands and you can find them established still in some areas, with their toes tucked well down into the chalk, limestone or clay soils. England, Wales and central Ireland can all boast of having *Primula veris* in residence (*see Figure 34*).

The plants have leaves which are typical of the Primulaceae family; oval in shape, pale green in shade and somewhat wrinkled, they differ from the primrose by narrowing, unexpectedly, half way down. Both the leaves and flower stems are downy, and the soft, pale down covers both sides of the leaves.

The golden yellow flowers are small and, with the green sepals, are shaped like elongated cow-bells. They grow in clusters and hang to one side of the stout stem and have been likened to a bunch of keys. Paigles or Peagles is the second name for the cowslip, and legend has it that Saint Peter dropped his keys somewhere in Europe and that where they fell so the first cowslip grew.

Nectar lies at the base of the long flower tube and only insects with long tongues can reach it. The cowslip, like the primrose, has devised a clever system of dual design in the arrangement of stamens and stigmas in its flowers, so as to ensure cross-fertilisation by some insects. The primrose, oxslip and the cowslip all hybridise and produce local varieties which can show differences in flower colour, for example, or in the hairiness of the plant.

In the small picture which has been made for you to copy, four flower heads have been used, but it is perfectly possible to make a similar charming one using only one or two; when you find cowslips growing in the wild they frequently produce fewer flower stems.

Pressing notes

Cowslips are easy to press, both the flowers and the leaves. Ensure that the bunches of small flowers are not too thick when you spread them on to the blotting paper. Either choose small heads or else detach some of the florets and press them separately, spreading out the remainder so that they press not more than one deep. Cowslips have thick stems and bulky leaves – make sure that you tighten the screws on the press regularly.

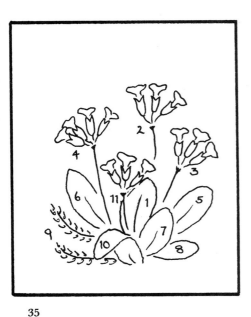

35

36 Pattern drawing from cowslip design.

Assembling the design

This familiar plant will give you very little trouble; it is quite robust, even when dried, and you should be able to handle it easily. Assemble your material and trim the stems until they echo those in the pattern and complement the leaves. Follow the numbers, finishing with a folded leaf to give the realistic foreshortening that you need to give depth to the picture. If you wish, you can add some small tufts or blades of grass to round off the design. Figure 14 shows the cowslip design in mid-construction, with a completed picture safely housed in an album.

DOG ROSE *Rosa canina* ROSACEAE FAMILY

Pink or white, five petals centrally notched and opening flat. Sweet scented with many golden stamens.

Five and sometimes seven leaflets, toothed round the edges. Thorns are curved downwards.

Hips are ovoid and shining scarlet, seeds inside are very hairy. Absence of sepals.

Height: 90–270cm (36–108in) clambers over hedges.

Habitat: Hedges and thickets, woods and on scrub – widespread except on mountains.

Flowering: June to August.

37

44

38 A dark, polished wood frame sets off the simple arrangement of dog roses and leaves, mounted on white linen.

The wild rose has, since Tudor times, had a symbolic association with the monarchy and our English history, and it must be one of the best-loved wild flowers in the country. There are many varieties, no fewer than 60 have been found and identified, but the one featured in the picture is probably the most common and, following a literal translation of the Latin name *Rosa canina*, is known as the dog rose. Why the plant originally attracted this unusual name is not clear, but there is no doubt that it has been used and appreciated for centuries, and is the ancestor of our garden rose. It grows abundantly in the hedges and thickets, arching over and threading through everything, with the flowers usually appearing towards the end of the stems. The pink or white flowers open wide, the five petals lying almost flat around the central boss of golden stamens. The thorns of *Rosa canina* are curved and exceedingly strong and sharp.

After flowering, as soon as the hips begin to grow behind each flower head, the sepals, as well as the petals, fall and the fruit swells, eventually becoming scarlet and shiny. Rose hips are an excellent source of vitamin C and are used to make rose-hip syrup.

The dog rose is widespread throughout the British Isles except in Scotland and, oddly, it is reputed never to be found growing on mountains.

Pressing notes
Try to eliminate all the very thick parts of the material you want to press before you put them on the blotting paper. Choose flowers which are freshly opened and trim away as much of the thick stalk and

45

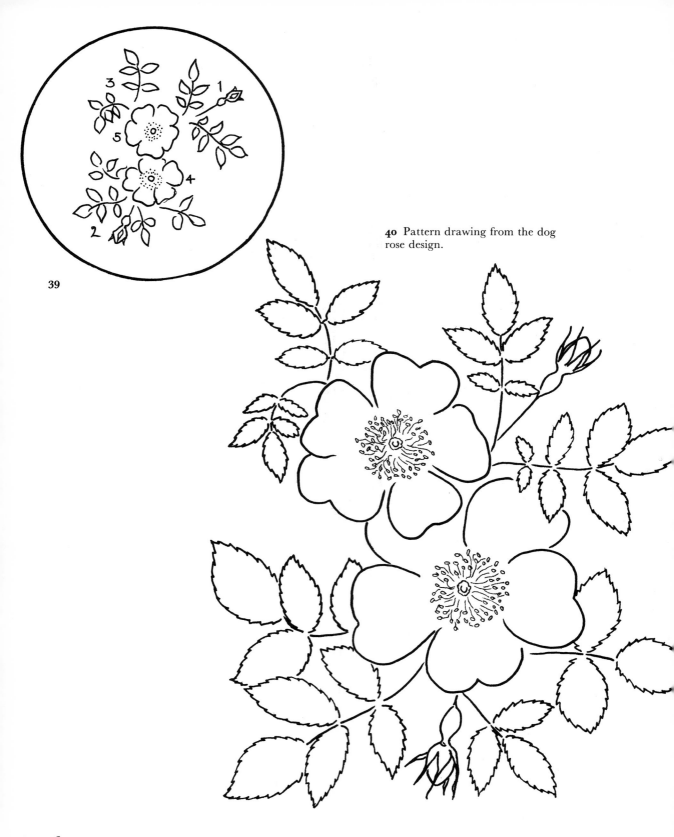

39

40 Pattern drawing from the dog rose design.

46

miniature seedbox from the back as you can. Choose buds which are small and divide them longitudinally with a razor blade. Detach the pairs of leaflets from the main leaf stem and press the latter separately with any other lengths of stem which are to form the centre line of the design.

Place the flowers and leaflets on one page and the half-buds on another, allowing plenty of space between everything. Make sure that all the flowers are completely dry before pressing; wild roses attract mould easily and the very slightest hint of this pervasive nuisance will destroy the faint, delicate colour of the petals. Allow plenty of time for the buds to dry.

Assembling the design

Follow the order as shown in the diagram, leaving the application of the two flowers until last. Try to make sure that there is a graceful continuation of line in the angle at which you place the leaf stems. Because of the thickness of these stems you will have to use a little more adhesive than usual; remember that this will mean that the picture must be lifted away from the pattern drawing (if you have used it) as soon as the design is complete. To illustrate how a design must be built around the natural curve of the rose leaves, the outline drawing shows a different arrangement to that in the photograph.

HEATHER OR LING *Calluna vulgaris* ERICACEAE FAMILY

Small mauvish-pink flowers on leafy, stalked spikes, loosely grouped. Sepals look like the petals and are the same colour. White variety appears occasionally.

Very small and stalkless, they grow in opposite rows and are narrow – linear – in shape.

Height: Short to medium shrubby plant up to 60cm (24in).

Habitat: Heaths, bogs and moorland, often covering large areas. Relishes poor acid soils.

Flowering: July to September.

41

Heather, or ling as it is often called, is an extremely strong growing plant that can carpet huge hillsides with its low shrubby growth and, when in flower, can bring glorious colour to the moors in summer months. It provides both food and cover for grouse and many other birds, while bees working through the heather flowers will produce an excellent scented honey. Ling was much used in olden days – dried out, the whippy twigs were useful in many ways to the crofters who lived and worked on the lonely moors in Scotland. To this day peat is still cut and used as fuel.

The little leaves are a fine fresh green in the early summer, and the flowers – not very much larger – are a pinkish-purple. The rather rare white variety can sometimes be found growing alongside its pink fellows and is well known for its reputation as a bringer of good luck.

Pressing notes

Pick and press sprigs and spikes which are freshly in flower. Old flowers

42

43 Pattern drawing from design of heather and grass of parnassus.

dry fawn. Pick off the side stems and press them separately especially if the flower spike is a thick one. Cut back any parts of stem which are brown and thick. Ling dries very well but treat it with care as by then the tiny leaves and flowers can drop off easily.

Assembling the design

This very simple design – a little ling, some grass of Parnassus and a fern or two – will be a reminder of summer and is ideal for placing in an album page with a peel-back plastic cover. They are sufficiently robust to withstand the slight pull of static, inherent in the plastic, which can upset more delicate material on the page when the plastic cover is replaced. Follow the numbering sequence and make sure that you trim the bottom of the stalks to a correct and comfortable length. When using an album with this type of page cover, you need not use an adhesive.

1 This large picture is full of summer flowers: poppies and scabious, chamomile and sweet scented lady's bedstraw, with some dark leaves of buttercup at the base.

2 Five flower designs in coloured mounts. The top left is of. sneezewort and grasses, while next to it is a firm little bunch of bluebells and primroses. The design in the centre is a 'peep-hole' picture and is a reminder of springtime. The bottom left arrangement shows pink and white yarrow, and the graceful bend of white bryony hanging from a wild rose completes the group. The dark mounts set off these wild flowers very effectively.

LADY'S BEDSTRAW *Galium verum* RUBIACEAE FAMILY

Bright yellow and very small, they grow in thick clusters and are sweet-scented.

Narrow and single veined, in a whorl of eight to 12 around the stem where branching takes place.

Height: 15–100cm (6–39in).

Habitat: Grassland, common on field edges, roadsides, banks and sand dunes.

Flowering: July to August.

The pretty yellow clusters of this summer flowering plant are sweet-scented, and when the plant is dried it still retains a pleasant aroma, which may account for the fact that it was used long ago as a bedding material. The name recalls the legend that Mary, mother of Jesus, lay on such a bed in Bethlehem.

   The plant is untidy and sprawling in its growth and can be found on banks and along the edges of fields as well as high on cliffs and dunes near the sea. Neither rough climate nor poor soil seem to deter this low-growing plant with its tiny leaves and flowers and fragile stems. The flowers are in thick clusters and at first sight would appear difficult to press. But, be bold, choose sprigs of modest size and press them whole. Lady's bedstraw dries quickly in the press and often emerges with the leaves and stems turned to a very dark green – sometimes almost black –

45 Pattern drawing from lady's bedstraw design.

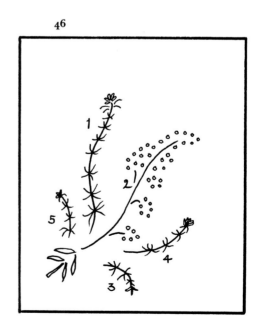

46

and this sombre yet delicate tracery can be very useful in flower pictures.

Many years ago people used lady's bedstraw medicinally to make a concoction to 'bathe the feet of Travellers and Lacquies, whose long running causeth weariness' – perhaps the modern jogger might find relief there too!

Pressing notes
Pick the smaller sprays – those that are freshly flowering – remove the larger side shoots and press them all, flowers, stems and leaves. The colours will all darken in the press. Material taken from small plants growing on poor, acid soil will turn almost black.

Assembling the design
This is a simple, straightforward design to make; simply follow the pattern drawing. The large picture on p. **oo** has lady's bedstraw in it and shows how useful this humble plant can be, especially for giving 'body' to the centre of a design.

LESSER CELANDINE   *Ranunculus ficaria*
RANUNCULACEAE FAMILY

47

Bright yellow, glossy petals eight to 12 in number. Star shaped, 2–4cm ($\frac{3}{4}$–1$\frac{1}{2}$in) across. Three green sepals.

Heart-shaped, rather thick and succulent with shiny surface. Sometimes blotched with darker or paler patches of colour.

Seeds clustered in achenes.

Height: Up to 20cm (8in) tall.

Habitat: Widespread on roadsides, banks, woodland and especially damp and shady places.

Flowering: March to May.

This small plant, the lesser celandine, can open its cheerful yellow flowers as early as March and at the end of a long winter they are indeed a lovely sight. Between March and May you will easily find this well-known plant growing beside paths and roads, in woodland and in gardens, thriving especially well in damp and shady places. In days gone by it was much used in herbal medicine, in 'Oyls' and 'Oyntments' and in 'Plaisters', but nowadays it has no practical use and gardeners are always keen to eliminate it from cultivated ground. The lesser celandine is, however, very efficient indeed in propagating itself, producing clusters of seeds in rounded seed-heads called achenes, as well as growing small bulbils at the base of each stem from which can emerge, the following spring, a new member of the tribe.

The buds and half-formed flowers are dark and greenish in colour but when they finally open to the sun, the yellow petals, which can vary in number from eight to 12, are glossy and shine up from the ground like bright stars.

The heart-shaped leaves are rather thick and succulent, the smaller ones sometimes held up on very long stalks. Occasionally the green, upper surfaces of the larger leaves are marked by either dark or pale blotches, but, whatever the colouring, they all appear smooth and shiny.

48 Celandines, some creeping cinquefoil leaves and three half opened ferns fixed over plain card and ready for your album.

The flowers of lesser celandine press very well and are most useful in flower pictures and, although they may fade to white in time, the starry shape will retain its glossy surface.

Unexpectedly, the lesser celandine is unrelated to the greater celandine, the former being a member of the large Ranunculaceae family and the latter belonging to the Papaveraceae family.

The flower design includes things which will be keeping the celandines company on the woodland bank: by mid-April the early ferns will be uncurling themselves and the silvery-grey leaves of the aptly named silverweed – *Potentilla anserina* – will be brightening the green of the grass. Both the shape and the bright colour of the celandines mean that they will mix happily with many other flowers.

Pressing notes

Lesser celandines are simple to press. Pick the flowers when they are freshly opened – old flowers turn white when they dry – and lay them both full-face and in profile on the blotting paper. Remember to pick buds and half-opened flowers, the small leaves and the larger basal leaves, and a few seed-heads if they are formed. The tightly curled ferns and the silver leaves must be placed to dry on separate pages in the press.

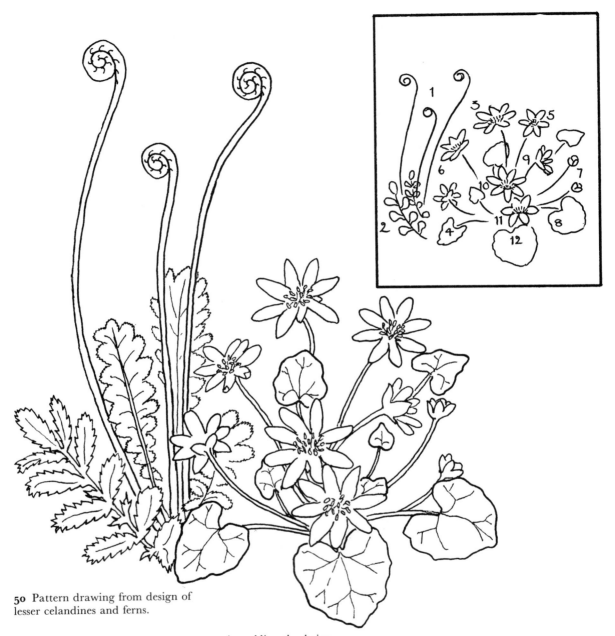

50 Pattern drawing from design of lesser celandines and ferns.

Assembling the design

Start with the ferns and the silver leaves and, after noting the overlapping in the diagram (*Figure 49*), add the celandine flower (number 3) and leaf (number 4) which link the two parts of the design together. Continue to add the celandine flowers and leaves, building up the picture of the plant and completing the design with the two full-face flowers (numbers 10 and 11). Note that not all the smaller buds and leaves have been numbered, but these can be added to complete the natural appearance of the plant to your own satisfaction.

ROSEBAY WILLOWHERB *Epilobium angustifolium*
ONAGRACEAE FAMILY

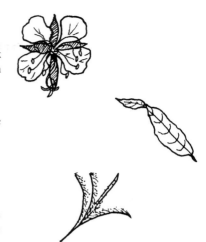

The four true petals are pink and slightly notched, sepals are dark purple and the stamens pale and long. Flowers are densely clustered on a tall spike and always face directly away from the central stem.

Leaves are long and narrow, the edges slightly wavy and toothed.

Long, four-sided capsule which splits open from the top. Seeds are plumed.

Height: Up to 120cm (48in).

Habitat: On waste ground throughout the British Isles. Very prolific.

Flowering: June to September.

The rosebay willowherb is a popular wild flower, despite its voracious ability to smother most other plants, and it owes its popularity to the beautiful pink and purple flower spikes which tower up in great banks of colour along the road sides. It seems to have a particular affinity for barren areas of waste ground, especially where fire has recently raged, thus giving rise to its country name of 'fireweed'.

This willowherb's efficiency at spreading itself is due to the roots, which burrow laterally, coming up above the ground every so often to start a new plant, and also to an excellent dispersal system for the super-abundance of seeds. The capsules split open from the tip and each of the four sections holds up its ranks of feathery plumed seeds to be caught by the wind.

Willowherb is used to good effect on the front jacket; although difficult to press well because of the size of the spikes, the bright colour is fully retained and, when combined with other flowers, such as meadow sweet, buttercups and ox-eye daisies, gives a happy reminder of a summer day. No wonder that another of its local names is 'queen of the meadows.'

Pressing notes

This is a difficult flower to press because of the size of the complete flower spike and the fact that the individual flowers grow all round the stem. Pick one which is going to fit into your press, hold the stem upright in front of you and, with a small pair of scissors, cut off the flowers which face directly away from you. Do the same with the flowers which face directly toward you and leave alone the flowers which grow outwards on either side and the unopened buds which run up to the tip of the spike. Detach in a similar fashion any leaves which cannot be accommodated to one side of the stem or the other and then place the trimmed stem on to the blotting paper. The remaining flowers down the sides of the stem will all press in profile as will the buds. Cut back the bottom of the main stem if it is very thick and encourage the tip of the spike to fall naturally on to the page, thus reinforcing any built-in curve.

Take a separate page of the press for the loose flowers and leaves. Take each flower and pinch it gently between your thumb and forefinger to persuade the small stalk at the back to lie straight, then place the flower face downward on the page. Try to remember how the

52 A single spike or rosebay willowherb.

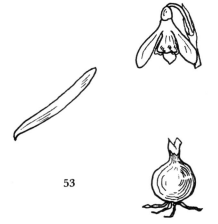

53

flowers faced you on the spike, and press some at a semi-profile angle (the ones in true profile are still attached to the stem). This will take time to do correctly but is always worthwhile – this willowherb presses extremely well.

Remember to press a few of the seed capsules, including one or two which are already split open – they are very decorative in shape and can be used effectively in other designs (*see Figure 4*).

Assembling the design

Despite the simplicity of the design in Figure 52 it requires some care and patience to re-form a flower spike so that it looks natural. Place the main stem first on to the page and, when that satisfies your eye, stick it down. Then assemble the loose flowers and place them so that they give fullness and a natural appearance to the spike. (Remember that the dark backs of the flowers should be upper-most on the page for those flowers which are behind the stem.)

Making this relatively small flower spike will give you good practice in re-forming a large clustered flower – only four full-face flowers have been pressed separately and added later.

SNOWDROP *Galanthus nivalis* **AMARYLLIDACEAE FAMILY (see p. 55)**

(see p. 55)

Pure white, the three large 'petals' are in fact sepals, the three shorter, true petals are inside and are edged with bright green.

Narrow and erect with a bluish-green bloom. 'Strap' shaped.

Round capsule.

Height: 15–25cm (6–10in).

Habitat: Woodland and shady places throughout the British Isles.

Flowering: January to March.

The snowdrop is one of the earliest plants to flower and even in a cold January you may find a few of these small, delicate flowers in a sheltered wood. The white flowers, with the short inner petals marked with bright green, are scented and hang drooping on their stalks, while the narrow, bluish-green leaves stand erect. Snowdrops form small bulbs and a single bulb will produce two or three leaves followed by one or two flowers during the first three months of every year, but, since they multiply quickly if left undisturbed, the tight clusters of bulbs will eventually put up large numbers of flowers. After flowering the leaves continue to grow longer and, finally, losing their stiffness and bending over, they give the plant an untidy appearance.

The name 'snowdrop' seems particularly apt when there is a cold spell of weather in February and the delicate flowers and leaves stand surrounded by snow; indeed, another country name for the plant links it with those inhospitable days – 'snow-piercer'. On warm sunny days, however, the gently nodding flowers will be a welcome sight for early foraging bees.

Snowdrops are probably not indigenous to this country but, having been first cultivated many centuries ago, they are now naturalised throughout England, Scotland and Wales.

54 The snowdrops and their leaves are growing close by some ivy and moss. This small picture will fit easily into most albums.

Figure 54 shows a clump of snowdrops and includes a small immature bud which has not yet tipped over on its stem to the typical 'hanging' position, while on the righthand side of the design there is a half-formed seed-head. Ivy leaves, a small tuft of moss and a shell-shaped piece of fungus complete the design and remind one of woods at this cold time of the year. Fungi can often be found growing out of old, fallen branches lying rotting amongst last year's leaves. (Any small arrangement of moss as well as ivy or other small leaves will be just as suitable for finishing off the base of this little picture.)

Pressing notes
Read through the general instructions on picking and pressing flowers and leaves on pp. 18-22. Snowdrops press well and are simple to lay head-to-tail on the blotting paper; no trimming will be necessary. Try to choose small, narrow leaves; their slightly curved surfaces will flatten outwards in the press and therefore broaden the width. Take a few of the leaves, fold them over at an angle and press like that; you will eventually need two like this to complete your design (see numbers 12 and 13 in Figure 55). The ivy leaves and small pieces of moss all press easily. The curved piece of fungus must be pressed separately but, despite its thickness, it will dry out easily. Place it between the pages of an old telephone directory and put a heavy weight on top.

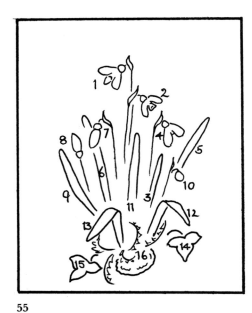

55

56 Pattern drawing from the snowdrop design.

Assembling the design

There are two points to remember when you make up this design. You may have to bend or cut the two leaves (numbers 12 and 13) artificially in order to achieve the effect that you need; make sure that you obtain the correct angle in order to achieve the foreshortening effect. The second point to remember is that you will need to use plenty of adhesive when fixing down the fungus – make sure that you lift the completed picture off the pattern page as soon as possible so that the adhesive can dry freely.

TRAVELLER'S JOY *Clematis vitalba*
RANUNCULACEAE FAMILY

Greenish-white, no real petals, rather stiff sepals and conspicuous bunch of pale stamens.

Three or five leaflets held pinnate in one leaf. The leaf stems twist around other shrubs allowing the creeper to climb.

Small brown seeds are held in cluster, each one grows a grey hairy plume. These woolly clusters often persist on the plant throughout the winter.

Height: Stem grows very thick and can be many metres in length, up to 30m (100ft).

Habitat: Common in southern England – less so in the north. Clambers on hedges and scrub, especially prolific on limestone.

Flowering: July to September.

Traveller's joy is a common sight in the hedges of central and southern England; it is a creeper and grows exuberantly over other trees and shrubs. The rope-like main stem can be as thick as a man's wrist and the plant climbs by twisting the stems of its leaves around the branches of its host. In the winter when the leaves have fallen, these tendrils look like corkscrews. It flowers in the summer time from July through the heat of August and September, and the greenish-white flowers and twisted tendrils have given it its true name *Clematis vitalba* or white vine. The little brown seeds each have a long feathery whisker and, when these are clustered together, they make great grey, woolly patches in the hedges and it is this which gives the creeper its other name, 'old man's beard'.

Pressing notes

Traveller's joy presses very well so long as you pick it when the weather is dry. It is thick to press and, because of this and its ability to retain moisture inside the flowers for some time after a shower, you should pick during only really sunny weather. If you are uncertain as to whether the flowers and leaves are dry before you lay them in the press, stand them for an hour (the bottom of the stalks submerged in a little water) in a warm dry atmosphere. Pick tips of the climbing stems, sprigs of flowers and separate leaves and press carefully, allowing plenty of space between each piece. Inspect the pages after a few days and discard any that show the slightest sign of mould; lift the remaining pieces on to a fresh page of blotting paper and re-press.

Assembling the design

Fix the flowers and leaves down in the usual way after you have studied the drawing. Choose one main leaf – if possible with the natural curve going the same way as the one in the design – and place it down centrally. Attach separate pieces of flower stalk and ensure that you place them so that they appear to be growing from the stem. If you wish to add a seed-head you must treat it with care – they easily come apart. Hold the seed-head in your tweezers and put a good-sized blob of adhesive on to, and also into, the centre of one side of it and spread it throughout the seeds as far as possible. Do not let the adhesive get on to

58 Pattern drawing from design of traveller's joy.

59

the feathers. Let it dry and then put a second and much smaller dab of adhesive in the middle of the first one; turn the seed-head over and place it on the picture.

WHITE BRYONY *Bryonia dioica* CUCURBITACEAE FAMILY (see colour plate 2)

Greenish-white distinctly veined, five petals. Male flowers (held in long stalked groups) are slightly larger than the female; they grow in different plants.

Five-lobed, shaped like an ivy-leaf. Tendrils grow out from the stem opposite to each leaf.

Berries, green or white when young turn to red when they are ripe. Poisonous.

58

Height: Climbing can reach 3m (10ft).

Habitat: Grows throughout the British Isles on well-drained soils, in hedges and on scrub.

Flowering: May to September.

White bryony is a member of the Cucurbitaceae family and so is related to gourds, the cucumbers and the vegetable marrows. Like them it grows very fast in response to a warm sun and, using strong tendrils, it can clamber up and over a hedge very rapidly. From May until late August or September the plant is all shades of green. The flowers – small female ones on one plant and the larger male types on another – are greenish-white with darker green veins; the leaves, roughly triangular in shape with five distinct lobes are matt green and numerous and the young berries also are green. But later, in the autumn, the berries turn scarlet and are a bright addition to the dying hedgerows.

The plant is a most efficient scrambler, the numerous tendrils will curl and twist around anything they brush against so that as the growing tip of each shoot grows upwards towards the sun the tendrils clasp and maintain its path over the hedge. This is a very common plant but, despite the similarity of name, it is not related to the black bryony.

The small piece of burnet rose in the design is a reminder of how the white bryony will clamber over its neighbours in the hedge (*see colour plate 2*).

Pressing notes

Picking a suitable piece of this plant can be time-consuming, as the tendrils often have to be untwisted in order to release the stem and, as can be seen from Figure 7, they are delicate despite their ability to twine. Once you have unwound them and freed the whole length of stem, cut it off and lay it on the blotting paper page, allowing it to curve naturally. Detach any flowers and leaves which, if pressed as they are, would lie across the main stem, and lay them on their own to press separately. Disentangle the tendrils and persuade them to curl and lie away from the stem. Press down with your thumb on any leaves remaining attached to the stem to encourage them to lie flat. White bryony takes up a great deal of space in the press and should never be crowded.

Assembling the design

Once you have chosen and trimmed to the correct length a piece of stem which will curve most naturally down the page over the pattern, you should fix it in place with adhesive. Let the base dry away from the pattern drawing and then replace it and take your time to choose and stick down the various leaves, flowers and extra tendrils. Take care to use a very little adhesive, especially when touching the tendrils – a slight smear at the thickest end and another just where the twisting begins is usually sufficient.

60

WILD THYME *Thymus drucei* **LABIATE FAMILY**

Small pink florets with purplish sepals are held in dense flower heads on short upright branches. Scented.

Small with prominent veins underneath and sharp bristles around the edges. Growing in pairs along the stem. Strongly aromatic when crushed from the oil glands located on the surface.

The stem is four-sided and hairy on two sides opposite to each other.

Height: Grows up to 7.5cm (3in).

Habitat: Dry grassland – especially on dunes and heaths.

Flowering: May to August.

The small creeping plant of wild thyme with its rounded, dense flower heads of small pink flowers is one of the best known of the true herbs of culinary fame. The oil which gives out a strong, distinctive aroma, comes from glands in the small leaves. In Tudor times, when herbs of sweet scent were much used to cloak the more noxious ones of everyday life, thyme was said to 'perfume the air most delightfully'.

It grows on open, windy places, enjoying the dry turf of cliffs, dunes and heathland, and is much loved and visited by bees. Another name for this little plant is 'mother of time'.

Thyme grows close to the ground and, left to itself, will put out short runners, gradually increasing its circumference until it forms a tight mat of growth. Two unusual factors are worth noting: the short stems are four-sided, two opposite sides being hairy and the other two being smooth, and the diminutive leaves are very sharp with tiny bristles along the edges.

62 A creeping piece of wild thyme and a short sprig of sheep sorrel and low grass.

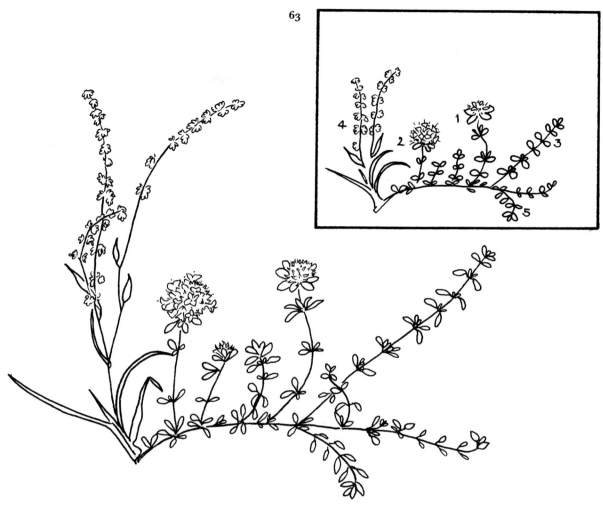

63

64 Pattern drawing from the wild thyme design.

Pressing notes
Pick and press a few complete lengths of the prostrate stems with the small upright stems rising from them. Add a few pieces of leafy stem and try to find flower heads which have not been open too long. Lay all the material flat on the page. Thyme presses well and quickly.

Assembling the design
The design made for you to copy is exactly as the plant would grow. Thyme invariably grows in the same gently curving fashion and it should not be difficult to find pieces to complete the picture.

65

WOOD ANEMONE *Anemone nemorosa*
RANUNCULACEAE FAMILY (see colour plate 3)

Pure white and star-shaped 20–40mm ($\frac{3}{4}$–1$\frac{1}{2}$in) across. The six to 12 'petals' are actually sepals. Stamens in a central ring are gold-yellow. Flowers and buds are often tinged with pink or lilac.

Whorls of three leaves, half-way up the straight stem are palmate, deeply divided into three segments and tooth edged. Single secondary leaf grows direct from rootstock at the end of the flowering season and is less deeply divided.

Cluster of seeds in an achene.

Height: 15–30cm (6–12in).

Habitat: In open clearings or on the edge of woods and coppices.

Flowering: March to May.

As their name suggests, these plants grow in woods and coppices. Beside a path or in a clearing where the spring sunlight can reach them freely you may find large groups of them. Each straight and springy stem holds up a fan or whorl of three leaves and, arising from the central point, comes a single flower – the whole growing as tall as 25–30cm (10–12in). The flowers are star-shaped and usually white, although there are also local variations in colour which show in a pink or lilac blush, especially deep in tone on the outside of the petal-like sepals and on the buds. (The leaves of the coloured varieties have a purplish tinge to them.)

The country name is 'wind flower' and the slightest puff will ripple the leaves and shake the white flowers. In the evenings when the sun begins to go down, or on cloudy days, the flowers close up and hang their heads, but on a sunny day they shine up from the green background of their leaves like bright stars, the thick ring of stamens making a golden centre to each flower (*see colour plate 3*).

Wood anemones grow out of small dark rhizomes which lie not far beneath the surface of the ground; once the flowers have fully opened, the thick root stock will put up a further single leaf of more substantial shape. The plant is sometimes labelled as poisonous and this is due to the nature of its sap – especially in the root; however, unless you should boil it up and drink it, it is unlikely to harm you and the rather unpleasant scent from crushed leaves alone will probably dissuade you before you experiment too far!

Pressing notes

The flowers close very quickly after picking, so take the press to the plant if you can. Cut the stalk away from both flowers and leaves and press separately. Remember to pick one or two of the single root leaves as well. Wood anemone presses very well and will dry quickly, but the flowers will then be extremely fragile. When lifting them from the blotting paper, take great care, first gently bending back the paper away from the petals to free them and only then sliding the tweezers under the central boss to lift them off. (Try lifting the least successfully pressed flower off first – learn on that one!) Flowers and leaves can be pressed together on the same page of blotting paper.

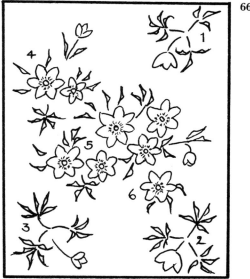

Assembling the design

The flowers of wood anemone are often semi-transparent when they are dry and this means that they will probably need backing before you can use them. This is not difficult to do and only requires a little time, patience and a steady hand. You can either place one flower on top of another and stick them lightly together, ensuring that both have the same number of petals, are roughly the same size, and that any extra 'frill' of the 'petticoat' flower is cut back, or you can back a single flower with thin white paper and again trim it back with scissors so that it is invisible from the front. More detailed instructions are on p. 22. Remember that in both cases you only need the smallest dab of adhesive placed centrally to stick flower to flower or flower to paper.

The numbered guide (*Figure 66*) shows you how the picture was constructed. You may prefer to let your own leaves and flowers determine the arrangement, always keeping in mind the loosely-knit appearance of these graceful plants.

5 Designs With Mixed Flowers

In this chapter you will see how you can make designs with your pressed flowers which extend beyond the straightforward naturalistic style which governed those in the previous chapter. There, only one flower was highlighted at a time and each small picture portrayed its plant as it would grow in the wild. In this second group, however, artistic licence has partly taken over and although the flowers and their own style of growth have been taken into account, it is the beauty of the mixed colours and the combination of the differing shapes of leaves which have inspired the pictures. Sometimes extra wild flowers outside the basic list of 33 (*see p. 15*) have been added to the pictures and you will come across gorse, bog asphodel, ragwort and honeysuckle to name but a few. None of these new flowers is uncommon or especially difficult to find and identify.

Each of the mixed designs will be illustrated by a photograph, some will be fixed on to plain card ready for inclusion in an album, others will be surrounded by a coloured border or mount, while the rest will be secure in picture frames. For the flowers used in the arrangements which are from the selected list, there will be the usual short botanical details and further information in chapter 7. There will also be general notes on the design, the background, the mount or frame, some advice on pressing and guidance about the construction.

The order in which the designs follow one another in this chapter is based on their complexity so that the first one featuring sneezewort is not difficult while the picture of poppies and scabious towards the end will be more time consuming and harder to complete. You will be able to make them using your own pressed flowers following method 3 (*see p. 31*) and using the numbered diagrams.

SNEEZEWORT (see colour plate 2)

This picture gives an austere impression – the colours are neutral and the green background and brown mount reinforce this feeling. Sneezewort flowers often grow in areas where grasses and rushes abound and the collection of the long stalks gives a true impression of the height of this quite tall plant. When choosing grasses to accompany the sneezewort make sure that they are not too large and flowing in shape, and simply aim to include ones which are of visual interest (botanical accuracy may have to be set aside!)

67

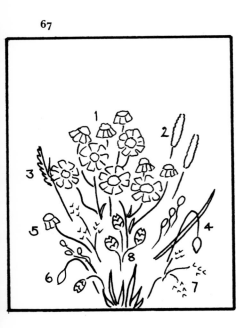

It is the botanical name which gives the clue to the unusual name – *ptarmica* comes from the Greek word for sneezing. But despite the unattractive English name it is one of the few wild flowers whose white petals retain their purity of colour in the press. Cut some of the flower heads from the stems and press separately. Choose grasses which have not been too long in flower.

68

Follow the numbers and let the stems run down untrimmed behind the bottom edge of the border. Do not overcrowd the flower faces.

SNEEZEWORT   *Achillea ptarmica*   COMPOSITAE FAMILY

White ray petals and greyish-cream centre of disc florets.

Narrow and lance shaped, sharp-toothed on the edges. Dark green and stem upright.

Height: 20–60cm (8–24in).

Habitat: Damp grassland mainly on acid soils.

Flowering: July to September.

WILD STRAWBERRY

This picture is different in that no attempt is made to copy natural growth and the main point of interest is the effective use of a black background. The black card throws into relief the silvery-grey thistle

69 Wild strawberries, a little cudweed and some creeping cinquefoil leaves are mounted on black card and put into a pale brown mount ornamented with two finely inked lines.

leaves and fuzzy flowers of cudweed in one corner and the four bending leaves of the humble, creeping cinquefoil in the other. The rigid placing of these two groups is divided by the wild strawberry plants; the overlapping and thickness of its leaves, flowers and fruits suggests perhaps that it is at the end of a row of strawberry plants in a vegetable garden! Work on both the corners first, arranging the strawberry leaves next, and finally tucking in the flowers and fruit.

The mount is a toast brown, neatly cut, with two black inked lines around it. All the material used in the design presses easily, the cudweed grows on bare arid ground, and the creeping cinquefoil is only too prevalent in grassy places. Turn the tiny thistle leaves the wrong way up for the silvery effect. The strawberry is easy to press and the small curving stems with the flowers and pendulous half-formed fruit lie easily on the page.

WILD STRAWBERRY *Fragaria vesca* ROSACEAE FAMILY

White, usually five-petalled with central boss of stamens.

Three leaflets on long stalks. Paler underneath. Puts out runners which form tiny new plants.

Fleshy fruit turning scarlet – surface covered with achenes.

Height: 5–30cm (2–12in).

Habitat: Woods, grasslands and banks – widespread.

Flowering: April to July.

YARROW AND GRASSES (see colour plate 2)

In this picture there are only five pieces of pressed material but their position both in relation to each other and within the green border is important.

Yarrow is in the same family as the sneezewort and the tiny flowers have the same construction: the ring of ray flowers surrounding a tiny group of disc ones. The flowers are grouped together in flat-topped clusters and their colour may be white, pink or a dingy half-way shade. Both the white and pink varieties are in the picture.

The grasses have been chosen for their colour, the very pale green shades help to accentuate the darker, feathery leaves of the yarrow and

71

so make the two flowering stems the focal point. Despite their sturdy shape, the yarrow presses very well; you should choose heads which are not too thick and remove only leaves which are very large. The background is white drawing paper and the mount cut from inexpensive, matt card.

Touch each piece with adhesive in three places. The spreading grasses should be fixed but the tips of the side stalks fixed last of all. Allow the stems to run down behind the mount.

72

YARROW *Achillea millefolium* COMPOSITAE FAMILY

White or pink, five ray flowers around a yellow disc centre. Many flowers held in flat heads.

Much divided with numerous small leaflets branching outwards. Dark green, aromatic. The stems are stiff and slightly downy.

Height: 15–45cm (6–18in).
Habitat: Fields, roadsides, hedges and wasteground – very common.
Flowering: June to November.

GRASSES

Grasses can be used most effectively in fresh flower arrangements and, when pressed, they can be equally decorative in a picture. In the back jacket illustration a number of different grasses have been pressed, shaped into a bunch and tied in the manner of an old fashioned sheaf with a twist of hay, then mounted on a bright background. Their delicate tracery can be seen to be very beautiful. Grasses on scarlet satin sounds an unusual mix but it is a question of opposites making a good marriage. The pale cream of the grass is thrown into strong relief by the boldness of the red and its satin smoothness makes the rough feel of the grass come alive. In fact, once you have appreciated that the pale colours and variety of outline require a dark, strong background to enhance their delicacy, then you have a wide choice of colour for it and you can mount on dark green, chocolate brown, deep blue or even a vivid purple.

73

By the end of the summer you should have a fair selection of grasses in your store and may be able to include some collected on holidays. At first sight it would appear that the bunch of grasses has been assembled in the hand and then laid down on the background but in fact it has been constructed stem by stem. Choose the main central grass and place it on the background. Decide where the bottom of the design is going to finish and trim the stem. Stick this single grass in place, leaving the end of it free, and then slowly construct the shape around it. Although a few more grass stems run straight down through the 'tie', most of them will need to be cut at this point and the resulting two pieces fixed separately. Stick down, with the minimum of adhesive – especially on the delicate flowers of the grass. Make a small twist for the 'tie' composed of eight or nine fine grass stems, fold them into a small loop, tie it with cotton and slip it under the few loose grass stems and up into the correct position. Apply a little adhesive at the back and press it firmly into place. Complete the picture by fixing in place the rest of the stems.

The gold and black frame is made from an inexpensive narrow moulding and does not overwhelm the simple nature of the pressed material.

SCABIOUS AND MUGWORT

Blues and greens arranged together can be unexpectedly pleasant and this small bunch of devil's bit scabious and tight mugwort flowers lies happily on an oval of blue silk, and the matt-green mount with an angled white edge frames the whole thing well.

The devil's bit scabious is said to have gained its curious name because the Devil, furious at the good, healing properties of the plant, pulled one out of the ground and bit off the end of the root in his rage. These days, however, nobody is interested in the possible benefits to be gained from eating scabious – except caterpillars!

It is a plant of spare appearance, the bright, blue buttons held on upright stems and it is the exact opposite in mode of growth to the mugwort. This extremely common roadside plant is pyramidal in shape and rather blowsy in style, with a great number of floppy leaves. As you pass in your car it appears uninteresting in colour, but a closer look will show you small soft flowers which are composed entirely of

74 The mount is a soft shade of mid-green and the background of silvery pale blue. Scabious and mugwort repeat these colours.

75

yellow disc florets (this is one of the unusual group of flowers which entirely lack the ray type), and the leaves are a beautiful shape, dark green on one side and a silvery grey underneath. The whole plant is aromatic and it was used at times in the past to flavour beer, instead of the more traditional hops. It is especially useful in making pressed flower pictures and the leaves by themselves will make a graceful design as can be seen in Figure 20.

The flowers in the picture are laid on the satin side of a pale blue dupion and are bunched together as if they had been picked on a summer's walk and carried home to a vase. Arrange the scabious flowers first on the background. Trim most of the stalks back to where the mugwort lies. Add the mugwort flowers and leaves and place centrally in the mount.

76

DEVIL'S BIT SCABIOUS *Succisa pratensis* DIPSACACEAE FAMILY

Flowers are small, purplish-blue, all of equal size, tightly packed into a round head. Held on slender stems.

Long and slender, sometimes the green blotched with purple.

Height: 15–100cm (6–40in).

Habitat: Damp and grassy places. Widespread.

Flowering: June to October.

MUGWORT *Artemisia vulgaris* COMPOSITAE FAMILY

77

Small florets grouped at ends of side branches. Yellow disc florets only.

Dark green above and silvery-grey underneath. Stems are reddish.

Height: 60–120cm (24–48in).

Habitat: Roadsides and waste places. Widespread.

Flowering: July to September.

FORGET-ME-NOTS AND MALLOWS

The forget-me-not is both a well-known and well-loved plant – its small flowers uncurling at the tips of the stems are usually the clear blue reminiscent of summer skies. There are several different forget-me-nots growing in our countryside – the common forget-me-not, the field and the water varieties – and you can use any of them to make this picture. There is a sentimental story emanating from central Europe, near the Danube, of how a medieval knight, in attempting to collect some of these blue flowers for his lady, missed his footing and slipped into the fast flowing river, calling out to her as he sank that she should not forget him. Since then it is claimed that the name forget-me-not has been given to *myosotis* which has always been held as a symbol of true and faithful love.

The mallow flowers which share this picture dry a delicate mauve – paler than their true shade when growing – and they make a colourful pattern with the forget-me-not. Tucked into the centre of the bunch are two pieces of pink yarrow and the mallow leaves, and the round 'cheeses' of the seed capsules complete the design, with no pretence to

78 An ideal design for your album, the transparent base material can easily be fixed down on to the page. The pale blue of the forget-me-not and the mauve of the mallows are delicate.

79

80

show anything other than the graceful lines and pretty colours of these flowers. Follow the numbered guide. This is constructed in three stages – the forget-me-not, the mallow flowers and the yarrow and small leaves. The mallow flowers dry paper-thin and require very careful handling; if they have faded badly it is worth 'doubling up' each flower by placing one above the other. The other alternative is to mount each flower face on to a slip of mauve tissue-paper, trimming away the surplus (*see p. 22*). The design is mounted on drawing paper and intended for inclusion in an album.

FORGET-ME-NOT *Myosotis arvensis* BORAGINACEAE FAMILY

Blue, five-petalled with yellow ring in the centre.

Stalked leaves in a rosette at the base of stem, leaves branching from stem are stalkless.

A hairy plant.

Height: 15–30cm (6–12in).

Habitat: Woods, bank and cultivated land. Widespread.

Flowering: April to October.

COMMON MALLOW *Malva sylvestris* MALVACEAE FAMILY

81

Five petals, colour ranging from pale to dark purplish-pink. Flowers grow in clusters of two or more. Petals are narrow at base and are purple veined. Stamens held in a protruberant boss.

Often five lobed, tooth-edged sometimes with a dark spot.

Capsules are solid, rounded – often called 'cheeses'; hold small ring of dark nutlets.

Height: 30–90cm (12–36in).

Habitat: Very common on roadsides and wasteground.

Flowering: June to September.

PRIMROSES AND BLUEBELLS *(colour plate 2)*

What child has not picked a small bunch of these flowers in spring and carried them home with care? April 19th is Primrose Day, the bluebells with also be coming into flower then and it will be a good time to pick the flowers and leaves for your picture. Cut the bluebells carefully and press them in profile – the leaves of the bluebell dry an unusual yellow shade, becoming translucent, and are therefore difficult to use in designs.

The primroses press very successfully; in profile they can simply be laid straight on to the blotting paper, but the ones which are to be pressed in full face should have the long tube of sepal cut away first.

Collect together a few grasses and leaves with your flowers and primrose leaves and assemble the design carefully, following figures 82 and 85, leaving the stalks until last. Cut off the stems at the 'waist' of all except the most central pieces and stick down last of all. The little brown flowers on the left of the stems are from a copper beech tree and the rounded heads and freshly opened brown leaf are unusual. Notice that the folded primrose leaf on the opposite side of the arrangement gives a depth to the whole collection.

82

Before you start to make up this design, give yourself a selection of primrose 'faces' to choose from. Flowers – especially when they are pressed full-face – acquire an 'expression' that can, in an indefinable way affect the whole aspect of a picture. Some seem to gaze upwards as if determined to look only at the sun, others appear downcast or modest in stance while a few can look downright disagreeable – one can see this especially in pansies and violets. Choose flower faces that will complement each other as well as filling the centre of the group. Primroses are better if they are 'backed' before use, and you will need to read the advice given in Chapter 2 carefully before you start. The flowers and leaves are placed on plain white drawing paper; the green mount makes a good border and the completed picture could be easily stuck into your album.

83

PRIMROSE *Primula vulgaris* PRIMULACEAE FAMILY

Five petals, pale yellow held up on long hairy stalks, deep yellow marking in the centre. Scented.

Leaves are wrinkled, light green and toothed at the edges, gently tapering to the stalk.

Hairy on undersides.

Height: Up to 15cm (6in).

Habitat: Woods, hedges and banks and grassy places. Widespread.

Flowering: March to May.

84

BLUEBELL *Endymion non-scriptus* LILIACEAE FAMILY

Azure blue, bell-shaped flowers hanging to one side of stem. Scented. (Occasionally white or pink flowers).

Linear with a 'keel', all springing direct from the top of a small white bulb. Leaves are fleshy.

Oval-shaped capsule, the seed black and shiny.

Height: 20–50cm (8–20in).

Habitat: Woods, coppices, banks – often carpeting considerable areas.

Flowering: April to June.

BEECH *Fagus sylvatica*

Familiar large trees. The leaves are pointed, oval in shape, and when they first uncurl they are silky underneath. The male flowers in March and April hang down in a rounded tassle and are also downy. Both the copper and ordinary beech provide good material for pressing.

DAISY AND BUTTERCUP CHAIN (see back jacket)

Children and their parents must have picked these much loved flowers and made them into necklaces or chains for centuries. To make a slit in the stem with your thumb nail and to thread the next flower through is a country pastime of great antiquity. And the idea can be repeated with pressed specimens to make a delightful entry in your wild flower collection.

Buttercups and daisies grow everywhere and allowing for the fact that there are several different varieties of the former in Britain, there will be one buttercup or another in flower from March to October and a late running autumn or a warm patch in early spring will extend this period. Daisies belong to that remarkable small group of plants which flower practically the whole year round, so there should be ample opportunities between March and October for you to pick and press. Both plants press easily. The bright yellow of the buttercup will eventually fade to white, but the petals retain their high polished gloss and so will still be effective in any design.

Most of the buttercups in the design are the bulbous buttercup and you can see the sepals turning downwards behind the petals, but the

3 The largest picture in the gold frame holds a wide collection of yellow and orange flowers: montbretia, gorse, broom and honeysuckle are all there. The small circular picture has only two flowers, thrift and daisies, growing, as they often do, close together. The bottom left-hand picture is a bird's eye view of wood anemones, while the cow parsley and marguerites in the next are a reminder of the lush growth of early summer. The small flower card holds a tiny collection of miniature florets and grasses.

4 This garland includes flowers, leaves and seed-heads spanning most of the year. The flowers lead down on either side from the pair of spring squills to meet where the sweet-briar roses overlap. Only the smallest flowers and buds have been used with a wide variety of grasses, ferns and leaves. Ivy-leafed toadflax and fennel, fuchsia and marjoram, primrose and willowherb, may and grass of Parnassus are all to be found here. It measures 30cm (12in) high.

85 Pattern drawing from the design of primroses and bluebells.

largest flower is a meadow buttercup – *Ranunculus acris* – and, although very similar, it has sepals which are erect and lie close to the petals.

The botanical name of the buttercup – *Ranunculus* – is derived from the Latin word *rana*, a frog, which underlines the fact that both plant and animal have much affection for wet and 'plashy' places. This decorative wild flower is poisonous to cattle but fortunately most cows seem to dislike the scent and to avoid them.

Daisies are so well known that they need little description; sturdy and low-growing, they set themselves up in small colonies on our lawns to the despair of keen gardeners. When the sun goes in and it is cloudy, as

86 A buttercup and daisy chain. The background is pale green, the pale cream of the mount leads on to the deeper shade in the wood frame.

well as in the evening, the white disc petal-like florets fold over the yellow centre of the flower and daisies get their name of 'day's eye' for this reason. It is a typical compositae daisy shape and the disc florets in the yellow boss are especially tightly packed – as many as 250 in a single flower. Daisies grow everywhere and by their low growth they can survive attacks by grazing animals and lawn mowers.

Although this is a fairly simple design, it is surprisingly difficult to make the chain truly circular. Mark out a circle with tiny pencil dots, or by placing a ring of marker pins before you commence work.

MEADOW BUTTERCUP *Ranunculus acris* RANUNCULACEAE FAMILY

Bright gold yellow, five petals all glossy (flowers occasionally pale yellow or white).

Divided into lobes – two to seven and all on same stalk. Green sepals are spread out but not downwards.

Numerous small, beaked fruits held in an achene.

Height: 30–90cm (12–36in).

Habitat: Damp meadows throughout the British Isles.

Flowering: May to October.

DAISY *Bellis perennis* COMPOSITAE FAMILY

Tightly packed yellow disc florets; surrounding white ray florets – often tipped with pink. Single flower on a stem. White petals close over the centre when the sun goes in.

87

74

Slightly hairy and spoon-shaped, they grow from a basal rosette.

Height: Low-growing and compact – seldom above a few inches.

Habitat: Everywhere, especially in short grass.

Flowering: All the year except in extremely cold weather.

88

COW PARSLEY AND OX-EYE DAISIES *(colour plate 3)*

This is a soft green and white arrangement designed purely to give the impression of a country road-side bank in May or June. The lacy abundance of cow parsley heads spread over a pale green silk remind you of the other popular name – 'Queen Ann's lace'. The dark green clusters of half-formed elder buds and pointed leaves seem embedded in the froth but they give a shape to the centre and lead in to the five faces of the ox-eye daisies. These big flowers are also known as marguerites and the yellow centres stand out well. A few heads of shaking grass have been added, the bulky shapes and soft colour adding to the design. This is *Briza major*, found nowadays as a regular garden escapee on waste tips and rubbish dumps. (Any single headed grass would fit into the picture just as well.)

First place the collection of cow parsley flowers on the background, and make up the design following the points of the compass plan. Add the elder flower buds and the two leaves, and finish with the big flowers and the few grasses.

The dark green mount and the gold bamboo frame repeat the shades and do not detract from the delicacy of the arrangement.

89

Pressing suggestions

Press cow parsley by cutting off a few complete flower umbels and laying some flat and some sideways. Remember to pick a few that are not fully opened and press them in profile as well as some leaves. Choose newly formed seed-heads which are still green. The material will dry quickly.

Select medium or small ox-eye daisies and cut away as much of the stem behind the bloom as possible – a collar may well help in pressing these thick flowers *(see p. 22)*.

Pick the tiny green buds of elder trees in little clusters and they will all darken in colour when they are dry.

COW PARSLEY *Anthriscus sylvestris* UMBELLIFERAE FAMILY

Tiny white flowers held in flat-topped clusters like umbrellas.

Finely divided in toothed segments – fern-like.

Small elongated fruits with small beak, held in clusters. Dries very dark.

Height: 60–120cm (24–48in).

Habitat: Banks and hedges, edges of woods and shady places also wasteland. Widespread.

Flowering: April to June.

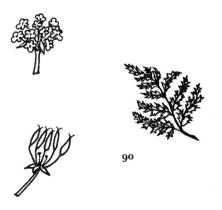

90

OX-EYE DAISY OR MARGUERITE *Leucanthemum vulgare*
COMPOSITAE FAMILY

Typical daisy shape, white and gold centred. Large – up to 50mm (2in) across single flower on upright stem.

Dark green and variable in shape and edging.

Height: 20–60cm (8–24in).

Habitat: Roadsides and all grassy places.

Flowering: May to September.

ELDER TREE *Sambucus nigra*

Very widespread growing along the edges of coppices, woods and roadsides. Flowers from May to July.

GREATER STITCHWORT, HERB ROBERT AND CELANDINES (*colour plate 2*)

The three wild flowers set in the circular mount are some of the best known in this country and you can find them growing along the banks and hedges bordering the roads and paths throughout the British Isles.

This is a 'peep-hole' picture and is simply meant to give you a glimpse of part of a roadside bank in Cornwall at about the time of year when Easter is at its latest. You can see the herb robert still leaning in its rather straggly way over the greater stitchwort. Although the latter has weak and brittle stems, it is growing up fast through the grasses towards the sun and, by leaning against its neighbours for support, it will overtake them, finally reaching 60cm (2ft) or more in height. At this point of its growth, however, each green group of buds is about to expand and grow feverishly upwards in a manner somehow reminiscent of those tightly packed Japanese 'flowers' which uncoil when dropped into water.

The fact that there are a few dark-petalled celandines here is a good reminder of how a wild flower can outrun its normal flowering season if the weather conditions have been unusual. An extended winter and a late spring will mean that some plants will be two or even three weeks late in their blooming.

Stitchwort is reputed to have got its common name because it was one of the main constituents in a herbal medicine made to relieve the pain you can get in your side known as a 'stitch'. The plant herb robert belongs to the family of geraniaceae and the name comes from the word 'geranos', a crane, because the distinctive shape of the pointed seed pod is similar in shape to the beak of that bird; this gives rise to the name 'cranesbill' by which it is often known.

All these plants will provide delicate material for your press and will dry unexpectedly easily and well. With a picture of this type you can easily add or substitute other spring flowers.

Make the design according to the numbered diagram (*Figure 92*) but referring continually to the mount. The stems must run down behind the coloured card. Peculiar to this design is the need to start work at the sides with the herb robert, adjusting their relative height very carefully, completing with the stitchwort and then adding the celandines and grasses.

GREATER STITCHWORT   *Stellaria holostea*
CARYOPHYLLACEAE FAMILY

White, five-petalled star shaped with the petals deeply notched.

Lanceolate and rigid with rough edges, growing in pairs almost direct from the angular stem.

Oval green capsule.

Height: 15–60cm (6–24in).

Habitat: Open woods, hedges and banks common throughout the British Isles. Enjoys shady places.

Flowering: April to June.

93

HERB ROBERT   *Geranium robertianum*   GERANIACEAE
FAMILY

Purplish pink, five-petalled flowers, usually grow in pairs.

Triangular but has three (occasionally five) distinct segments deeply cut. Stems are a little hairy – both parts turn red when old. Leaves give off unpleasant smell when rubbed between fingers.

Long beak-shaped capsule which breaks open from the bottom to top.

Height: 15–25cm (6–10in).

Habitat: Roadside banks, woods and stony places common everywhere.

Flowering: April to November.

94

CELANDINE (see p. 50)

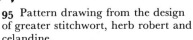

95 Pattern drawing from the design of greater stitchwort, herb robert and celandine.

96

THRIFT AND DAISIES *(colour plate 3)*

The circular design of thrift and daisies such as you might find on a cliff top is a good example of the combined botanical and artistic approach. Both are compactly growing, mat-forming plants and both can be found growing either near the sea or on mountains. However, it is unlikely that they would be formed naturally into so attractive a group without any intervening short-cropped turf, so it is here that your artistic eye can take over and expand and develop the low-growing charm of these two little plants until you have a picture to satisfy your eye – and one which will undoubtedly remind you of the place where you picked them. (In the old 'language of flowers', thrift means 'sympathy' and the daisy 'innocence' which should certainly prove an easy mix!)

Since you will be adding small clumps of plants, take care that you do not overcrowd the picture. Try to get the natural lines of growth in the dominant flower heads flowing through to the next plant. Use a little more adhesive than usual – and you can spike each clump with a pin to keep it in place until the glue dries.

Two sprigs of half-opened kidney vetch complete the picture.

Pressing notes

Both thrift and daisies are prolific in their growth and can afford to let you pick small side-shoots and tufts containing leaves, flowers and buds. It is easy to detach them completely and, since the bottom section of stem, where it meets the root, acts as a holding point, none of the leaves should become separated. Provided that the tufts are not too thick, simply press them outwards like a fan between your thumb and fingers and then lay them on the blotting paper – complete with flower and stem.

Press some extra flowers separately to ensure that you have enough of both full-face and profile flower heads for your needs and try to have as wide a variety of shade as possible – this will add to the interest of your picture.

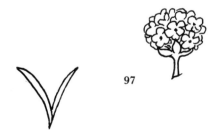

97

THRIFT *Armeria maritima* PLUMBAGINACEAE FAMILY

Pale or dark pink rounded clusters of small florets. Five sepals and brown bracts – papery. Held up on a single stem.

Linear, very narrow with only one vein. Low growing in tufts which form a continual 'mat'.

Height: Up to 15cm (6in).

Habitat: Dry grasslands, cliffs and mountains. Throughout the British Isles.

Flowering: April to August.

DAISY (see p. 74)

KIDNEY VETCH *Anthyllis vulnaria*

This plant grows on the cliffs close by the thrift, flowering from June to September. The small pea-type florets are held in kidney-shaped clusters and can be found in a lovely range of colours: off-white and yellow, purple, and even orange or brick red. When the early flowering shoots appear on the plant they are silvery when dried (as can be seen in colour plate 3).

POPPIES AND CHAMOMILE *(colour plate 1)*

Scarlet poppies, with their attendant drooping buds and the seed boxes standing upright like stiff soldiers, must be one of the best known wild flowers. Garden varieties are often rather vulgar with their frills and big leaves, but the true field poppy that grows along the edges of the corn fields is quite spare and restrained in style and only the soft, scarlet petals are eye-catching. Sadly, the true colour changes when they are pressed, drying to a purplish red and so thin as to be almost transparent, but if they are mounted on red tissue paper *(see p. 22)* they regain some of their scarlet fire and you can use them in a picture like the one in colour plate 1.

Corn chamomile is another of the flowers listed on the flowering chart and it sometimes grows alongside the poppies; with its slightly scented leaves it, too, is a very pretty plant and presses well.

Combine poppies and chamomile and you have the beginnings of a summer picture. Complete it with blue scabious, a little yarrow and some lady's bedstraw, feather it round with grasses and tendrils and the memory is completed.

This fine old Victorian oval frame with the pale green mount encloses the whole picture in a charming manner, and the black accentuates the very dark buttercup leaves at the bottom of the flowers.

The poppy plant is amazingly prolific with its flowers and may put up hundreds during the flowering months. Each bloom only lasts for one day and then the petals – usually with a black blotch at the base – will fall and the immature seed capsule begin to swell.

Pick flowers early in the morning and press some full-face and some in profile; collect a number of buds and some half-formed seed capsules as well as a few leaves. Once the flowers have begun to dry, resist any temptation to move them; they are extremely fragile and, when you finally wish to lift them from the page, *bend the blotting paper back from them* and never try to pull the petals up from the page.

The corn chamomile has several relatives, notably the stinking chamomile and the scentless mayweed both of which will act as substitutes in this design if they grow more commonly in your area than *Anthemis arvensis*.

The field scabious is a tall plant which also grows in the fields and along roadsides and the blue flowers are great favourites with bees and insects.

This picture is a large one measuring 56 by 46cm (22 by 18in), and you may find it easier to make if you choose as a background a firm cotton or linen (backed with a piece of iron-on Vilene) rather than attempting to work on thin organdie mounted on card, as has been done in the illustration. Cut your background larger than the frame, place the mount on top to guide you and your choice of material beside you.

The tall central grass must set the pattern going and it must be stopped by the dark swirl of a leaf at the bottom. The poppy buds and seed-boxes can be added next to settle the width of the design and the outline can then be filled in with clear and interesting shapes. Decide where next you are going to place the poppy flowers and finish the outline with extra grasses. Add the yarrow and scabious and chamomile, letting the blue and white run through the bunch to form balanced lines of these two shades. Tuck in the rest of the material which you feel will enhance the summer feeling and extend the colour interest; for example the dark seeds of one of the umbelliferae repeat the dark shade of the poppy buds, and the touch of hedge parsley throws the white out towards the edge. Tendrils should be fixed last of all.

Only when you have made quite sure where every piece must lie should you stick everything down. There are two easy ways to help yourself remember where each piece goes. First, place a sheet of tracing paper over the design and roughly draw in the position of the larger and most important flowers and leaves and use this as a guide; the second tip is to stick an upright pin into the material to mark the place from where you lift a flower in order to apply the adhesive – then you can replace it with accuracy.

98

CORN POPPY *Papaver rhoeas* PAPAVERACEAE FAMILY

Two pairs of overlapping scarlet petals often with a black blotch at the base. Silky and fragile. Flowers last a single day.

Upper leaves are three-lobed and stalkless, the lower ones have stalks and narrow lobes. Stem and leaves are hairy.

Seed capsule almost round with a distinctive flat top. Very upright stem.

Height: 20–60cm (8–24in).

Habitat: Cultivated fields and roadsides. Also on waste ground. Uncommon in the far north.

Flowering: June to October.

CORN CHAMOMILE *Anthemis arvensis* COMPOSITAE FAMILY

Ring of white ray florets and centre of yellow disc type.

Delicate and finely divided. Slightly aromatic. Stem is erect.

Height: Up to 20cm (8in).

Habitat: Arable and waste land along roadsides. Rare in Scotland.

99

Flowering: June to September.

Other wild flowers used
Field scabious *Knautia arvensis*
Lady's bedstraw (*see p. 49*)
Yarrow (*see p. 67*)
Cow parsley (*see p. 75*)

A YELLOW PICTURE *(see colour plate 3)*

Another simple idea which can form the basis for a picture is to collect a group of flowers of one shade and then enjoy turning them into effective arrangements. Many wild flowers are yellow and this cheerful colour is grand to work with; you can mix them up with a collection of differing greens and browns, add a little orange of montbretia and surround it with a narrow gold frame and so make a striking picture. Honeysuckle, gorse, ragwort and broom, bright montbretia and agrimony, there are 16 different flowers here, with the green hanging tassles of stinging nettle perhaps the most unexpected. You will recognise some old friends from Chapter 4 – the coltsfoot, celandine, buttercups and bird's foot trefoil. Leaves, ferns and lichen have been chosen for their shape as well as their odd shades of green; a large group of flowers, none of them very big, requires a strong perimeter of unexpected shapes.

This type of picture will have to be made towards the end of your first year of pressing wild flowers. It will take time to collect a sufficient variety of material to fill a frame of this size which measures 40 by 35cm (16 by 14in).

Pressing notes

Most of the flowers will press easily but a few need special care. Honeysuckle is thick – choose small flower heads and press the little trumpets outwards into a fan, then shape with your thumb and fingers. It may well dry brown or at best a deep cream and is notoriously inconsistent in this respect. Gorse, too, is difficult to press, mainly because it is so prickly to handle and it requires one side to be trimmed of spines. After that, somewhat surprisingly, it presses quite well – but detach the biggest flowers and press them in profile separately. Fleabane, the yellow daisies with large buttons of yellow disc florets and a thin fringe of yellow ray ones, also needs heavy pressing. Do not overcrowd any of the thicker flowers on the page of the press. Ragwort presses badly and there seems no alternative but to lay sprays of it on the blotting paper and hope that a few will turn out well!

All the leaves are straightforward to find and to press, although the grey lichen will need disentangling, and small bunches will be best.

Assembling the flowers

This is essentially a picture where you should work inside the frame. Choose a neutral background of paper, card or a fabric of some substance and arrange first the outside circle of material, fixing the position of the compass points first, and then begin to work slowly inwards. Balance the colours as you do this and do not stick anything down until you are quite sure you have the whole design as you want it. Reach for the Copydex only when you are completely satisfied. (Refer back to the instructions for assembling the previous picture.)

This is a picture which you could easily construct by laying the material loose on the prepared background and then, dispensing with any adhesive, holding it in place by the pressure between the frame and the backing. The method for doing this is explained more fully on p. 35.

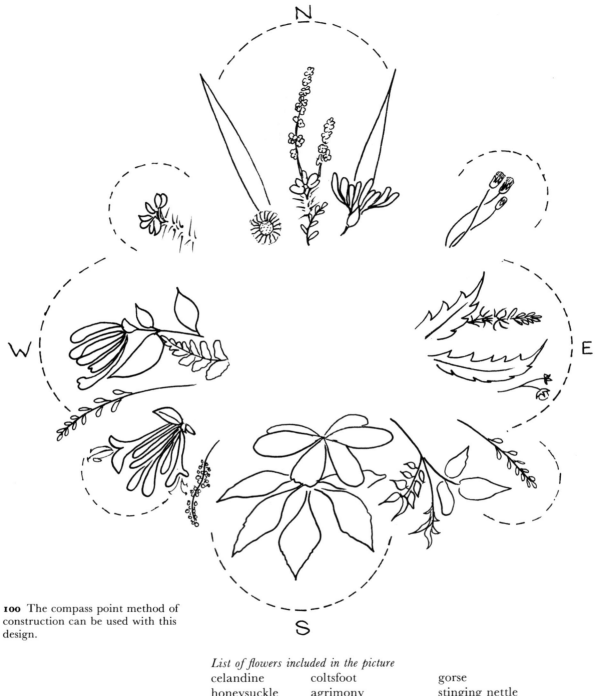

100 The compass point method of construction can be used with this design.

List of flowers included in the picture

celandine	coltsfoot	gorse
honeysuckle	agrimony	stinging nettle
fleabane	bird's foot trefoil	yarrow
ragwort	bog asphodel	reflexed stonecrop
montbretia	tormentil	buttercup
hawkweed	broom	

SUMMER ABUNDANCE *(see front jacket)*

The final picture in this chapter is one of mixed summer flowers and all 28 of them have been gathered up and arranged together in this lush fashion to show how varied and beautiful nature can be. Most of the flowers are indigenous and have grown freely throughout the British Isles for centuries. A few were imported years ago from distant parts of the world as garden flowers and have had their seeds blown over the garden wall to become members of that select tribe known as 'garden escapees'. The hanging red flowers of fuchsia are in this category as well as the two pretty white polygonums. Leaves of bramble and beech; tamaris and creeping buttercup; a fern laid the wrong way up to show the ripe brown spores; a dark curl of moss and some umbelliferae seed clusters . . . this long list only touches the surface of the extraordinary variety of shape and colour of our flora.

The meadow sweet which is found easily in the picture, is the last in the list of common wild flowers selected for special attention in this book. It grows throughout the country, flourishing in Scotland just as it does in Cornwall. In the height of the summer months of June to August when it is left undisturbed, it will grow and flower vigorously in meadows and on moorland, in ditches and on the banks bordering roads and rivers and will smother sizeable areas with the cream foam of its flowers. It is a lovely sight and has a sweet fragrance. In olden days it was one of the scented flowers which were strewn on the floor to help mask other more horrid smells.

By the time you have gathered together and pressed enough flowers to make a picture in this style, you will have gained a lot of experience both in pressing flowers and in arranging them within a frame. Before passing on to more ideas in the next chapter, here are a few points to remember:

Make the outline interesting and use the colour of the background material to help accentuate this.

Do not overcrowd the design in the frame – allow enough space around it to be comfortable.

Do not cram too many flowers into the arrangement itself – let some of the stalks be seen reaching down into the centre.

Make sure that there are some graceful lines flowing through the design.

Remember that placing light on dark and vice versa makes for great effect.

Dark colours usually need to be placed low down in the design.

MEADOW SWEET *Filipendula almeria* ROSACEAE FAMILY

Five cream petals and numerous long stamens. Five green sepals bent back.

Green above and white and hairy underneath. Pairs of small leaflets on the stem separate the larger pairs – up to five pairs and large one at the top. Tooth-edged.

Height: 60–120cm (24–48in).

101

Habitat: Common throughout British Isles. Wet parts of woods, ditches, marshes and moors; also fens.

Flowering: June to August.

Other flowers used in this picture

rosebay willowherb	ragwort
thistle	cow parsley
buttercup	ling
mallow	hawkweed
ox-eye daisy	Himalayan knotweed
bird's foot trefoil	elder flowers
fuchsia	slender St John's wort
fennel	field scabious
polygonum	feverfew
bell heather	hemp agrimony
traveller's joy	yarrow
hedgerow cranesbill	stinging nettle
bindweed	cow-wheat
meadow sweet	mignonette

6 More Wild Flowers and Special Pictures

The flowers which are featured individually in this book are only a small fraction of the huge population of what is commonly known as the flora of the British Isles. A glance at the index of a good comprehensive flower book will show you the extent of the list, for it will certainly cover several pages and include well over 1000 varieties. Common ones and rare ones, plants which grow in colonies and those that are loners, tall-stemmed ones and ones that creep on the ground – all these many-styled flowering plants are there to be found and appreciated by us when we walk in the country, although only a relatively small number can be recommended for pressing. This is not to say that pressing them all would not be possible. Think of pressing a foxglove in full flower – the thick spike of the stem adorned all around with 20 or 30 flowers and buds, the leaves at the base as big as a small frying-pan – anyone wanting to press such a monster would have to invest in an outsize press and take over a bedroom wall to mount the collage! It would seem sad to confine the fine flowering of large or bulky plants in such an operation and, only if it was done for a specific purpose, such as botanical identification perhaps, would it be worthwhile.

Pressing very diminutive flowers can be equally difficult. Soft and delicate plants like the chickweeds and the speedwells, for example, have fragile flowers and a growth pattern which seems to defy the press. Initial trimming and a most difficult reforming after they are fully dry is possible but, once again, it could be classified as a labour of love rather than one which will add useful items to your collection. If you are using your pressed flowers and leaves to make small pictures to further your botanical understanding, then all common flowers, however difficult to press, must be of interest. If, however, you are solely augmenting your 'artist's palette' with which you create your designs, then be selective in what you pick and press. Leave alone the modest and delicate plants, just as you should the very large or those of awkward shape – you will find that other flowers will serve just as well in your picture. If a plant, however common in other places, is unusual in your area – do not pick it. Achieving success in your picture-making is dependent on things other than the inclusion of particular wild flowers. Your eye must learn to look for and assess the beautiful shades and outlines that are already

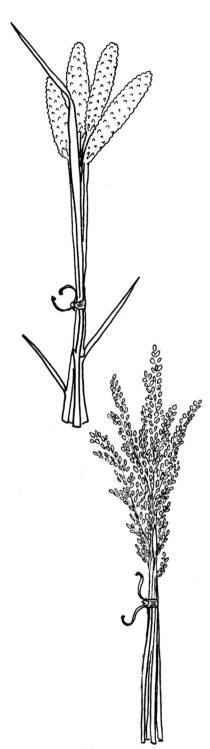

102 Two small bunches of grass heads tied with a piece of soft cotton.

available in the common flowers growing in your own part of the country. The wild flowers that feature in this book were picked throughout one year in Hertfordshire, Cornwall and a few days in Scotland.

The glossary on pp. 105–16 gives advice on which plants will press easily and be useful in pictures. Some of those listed will provide corolla or buds, for example, while others will offer only leaves and seed-heads. The Latin names are given throughout the list so that you can read up about the families and botanical details in your wild flower book.

Trees, too, can play their part in helping to fill your store of pressed material. The beautifully shaped silver leaves from the willow, or the dark leaves and soft flower bunches of the copper beech, press excellently. Another favourite is the lime tree with its scented, yellow-green flowers and the accompanying propeller leaf of pale green, while the common elder tree, so often found in hedges and at the edges of coppices, produces wide clusters of creamy florets and tiny green buds which dry almost black. All these and many more are listed, together with pressing notes and general advice, and it will encourage you to collect as wide a selection of material as you can all through the year.

A great deal of nature's abundance goes into the green foliage of plants, and many leaves can be pressed and used by themselves in decorative designs. Figure 6 shows the extraordinary variety between the leaf shapes of very common trees.

If you have already worked through Chapters 4 and 5, trimming and pressing your flower material as you go, then you will have gained experience in knowing which flowers will or will not press well. You will find that this knowledge will assist you to be selective when you find other flowering plants in the hedgerow. Experiment continually but only with a limited number of leaves, blossoms or buds each time.

We tend to think of flowers as brightly coloured in pinks or blues, yellows, purples or even combinations of two or more of these shades, but the sober tones of the flowers of grasses and rushes can be retained too when they are pressed and, when mounted on a well-chosen background, they can bring a surprising delight to the eye. The creamy grasses in Figure 102 are all laid on a gentle beige background and this highlights the delicacy of the minute florets on their thread like stems. Seed-heads are very hard to press successfully; by their nature they are well on the way to being both dry and brittle when you pick them, and a further sojourn in a warm press may well end in a suitably flattened container which has sprung open, correctly released its dry seeds and lost its shape. Try, therefore, to pick the capsules, pods or whatever type they may be, when they first form on the plant – the size will probably be immaterial as the young containers will still have enough definity of shape to be useful to you.

Ferns are particularly attractive when they are pressed – they retain their colour and, because of their simple, two-dimensional form, provide a most satisfying outline in a picture. Only the thick hart's tongue fern is unreliable; all the other common ones which you will find in the woods, beside streams and growing in old walls will reward your industry. The common green bracken will provide you with small pieces of tough, green fronds in the summer time, while in the autumn

103 A silver frame and a black mount surround the silhouette picture of cow-wheat, and moss. It measures 30 by 26cm (12 by 10½in).

these will have turned golden; finally, in early winter you will be able to collect small spirals and the curly tips of brown dead fronds. You will find ferns used in a number of the illustrations.

Mosses and lichens which inhabit damp shady places can supply you with unusually-coloured extras for your pictures. Tiny tufts of some mosses will dry a vivid green or a rich sienna-brown, while pieces of lichen, pressed firmly into manageable shapes, will retain their silvery-grey. Several of the flower pictures have little fragments of these low-growing plants included in them to help provide a reminder of the woodland habitats they frequent.

When you create designs with bright flowers it is the colour of the petals which is of first importance – the happy balance between the shades, or in the contrast of tone – while the shape and outline of the flower face seem to take second place. When you are making a picture using only leaves and ferns, however, that is all reversed. Now size, outline and shape govern your choice of foliage, while the colour of the background assumes greater importance in the planning of the design, for it must enhance and strengthen the tracery of the outline. The black and white of the picture in Figure 103 is dramatic and stark; cow-wheat and moss grow together in this manner in woods and, when dry, are still lifelike in stance and silhouette, despite the fact that the colour of the cow-wheat has changed completely. They illustrate well how only the shape of plants can be exploited in design.

Moorland in August, when the heathers are in their full purple, might well be another starting point for a picture. Bog cotton – those untidy white-tipped grasses – deserves a place in the design as well as the neat yellow spikes of bog asphodel. Perhaps you will have found some eye-bright or lousewort or even a little milkwort, and there is always the chance that you will have been lucky and come across a small bush of white heather. The two little pictures made for a small album (*Figures 104 and 105*) will remind you of where and when you picked the heathers (see also the back jacket illustration).

ALBUM PICTURES

When you are making pictures of this type, dispense with adhesive altogether and simply lay the pressed flowers and leaves down on to the page and cover them with the transparent second sheet.

The album will have its quota of detachable pages when you buy it and, although usually sold for displaying photographs, the prepared pages (each with a fold-back plastic skin) are excellent for showing and preserving your flowers.

Detach a page from the clip-rings of the album and have ready your choice of flower material and your tweezers. (It is advisable to plan your design on a piece of spare paper and then, when you have arranged it to your liking, transfer it to the album page.) Peel back the clear skin opening up the base page and begin your work by laying down the longest perpendicular piece of material on to the base so as to fix the position of the design on the page. Then settle the width to right and to left and finally complete the group, including all the different flowers which you want to show. Follow the north, south, east and west plan once again.

Place the material carefully on the base page; you will find that it feels mildly rough, almost tacky, to the finger tip and this will prevent the flowers from moving. It will also mean, however, that any minute particles detaching themselves from your material – for example, tiny ripe spores from the reverse side of ferns, dust or other unwanted fragments – will tend to adhere separately and can give your clean page a most spotted and grubby appearance. Blowing is no good at all – the top flowers will blow away and all the pernicious little miseries will stay put!

Despite this small hazard you will find it quite straightforward to construct your flower design. When it is finished, you must replace the clear top skin of plastic. Pick up the edge of the skin with the hand which is furthest from it. Slowly lower the skin over the flowers using the side of the thumb of your other hand to ease out air bubbles that can become trapped. Once it is safely lowered and the flowers fully covered then the whole page is ready to be returned to the album

The first moorland picture (*Figure 104*) is composed of two shortened stems of rush, some heather, a little blue milkwort and a couple of silvery leaves of alpine alchemilla. The single sprig of lousewort makes an interesting focal point – despite the fact that it has entirely lost its cheerful pink in the press.

The second page (*Figure 105*) shows a little collection of flowers which also grow on the moors and which have a special liking for damp and stony places. Small bells of cross-leaved heath join a spike of yellow bog asphodel which has finished flowering and is making its seeds. To the right there droops a trail of New Zealand willowherb and on the left side there is the fluffy bog cotton and a small plant of sundew – *Drosera rotundifola* – and the sturdy stem, complete with its forming seed-capsules form the centre of the plant.

When you have finished the designs and replaced the pages in the album, remember to list the flowers together with when and where you picked them and put this information in the back of the album.

104 Heather, lousewort, milkwort and rushes.

105 Bog cotton, heather, sundew and New Zealand willowherb.

Making pictures of this kind, where you are deliberately setting yourself restrictions as to a season, an area, and then a limitation in the number of plants, can be very rewarding. Interesting to plan and absorbing to create, they can either be kept in scrap-books or albums, made into calendars or cards or be framed and hung on the wall. Holidays, a special outing to the country by town-dwellers, a stop-off from the motorway for a picnic in a wood can all make small occasions to remember. A few flowers and leaves picked carefully and put as soon as possible into your press, with a note of the date and place, can be the beginning of a modest collection. It is a measure of the in-built beauty of wild flowers that you will find that the more you learn about them in the slow making of a small design the more you will enjoy them.

Not all small flowers are delicate to handle and many of them press very well. After pressing and working with your wild flowers over several months you will probably discover that you have collected a number of what the botanical books term 'low-growing' plants. Their modest size, however, can make them difficult to use in all but a few of your arrangements, as they are easily overwhelmed. (The oval design in colour plate 4 and Figure 10 shows how beautiful they can look.)

PATCHWORK PICTURES

It is worth considering a patchwork picture made especially to hold a certain number of these diminutive blossoms, and Figure 106 and the back jacket show how charming one can look. The whole picture is reminiscent of a Victorian sampler and a little embroidery reinforces this idea. A mixture of soft colours in the patchwork gives a background which accentuates the tracery of the small leaves and stems and never overpowers the fragility of the petals.

For making the picture you will need a small yardage of three different colours of good-quality cotton sheeting. Department stores should carry this household fabric and the range of shades is wide. Alternatively, any finely-woven cotton and polyester mixture will serve your purpose. You will also need a template, a metal pattern to guide

106 A patchwork picture showing 20 small flowers bordered by fennel and willow leaves. Included are Alpine alchemilla, scarlet pimpernel, spring squill, stonecrop, heartsease pansy, whortleberry and bramble.

you when you cut out first the paper shapes and then the patches. (Templates of varying sizes can be bought in shops that sell materials and have haberdashery counters.) The one used for this picture was of good quality, made of metal and 44mm (1¾in) in size, and it was sold with a window template.

Equipment and materials needed
A template – with or without a window template
About 6 sheets of A1 bank white paper
Fabric of three different colours
A Stanley knife
An old bread board or similar flat surface to cut on (old magazines will also suffice)
A good sharp pair of scissors
A ruler, pencil and pins

A roll of masking tape
Needles and thread both white and coloured
A small quantity of iron-on Vilene

1 Place a sheet of paper on the cutting surface. Put the template in one corner of the paper and cut round it with the knife. Cut out 20 full-sized paper shapes and a further 15 half-size shapes (for the edge).

2 Iron the fabric well. Plan out your colour chart now and mark the papers accordingly. Lay a paper patch on to the fabric; line it up with the straight of the thread and pin centrally. Cut out with the scissors, leaving about 1cm ($\frac{3}{8}$in) margin all round (if you have a window template lay that over the patch and mark around the edge with tailor's chalk and cut around this line).

Cut out the full-sizes patches, setting aside enough straight pieces of fabric to form a 'surround'. Cut the final part patches from the remaining material, following the colour chart, and centre pin each one.

If you wish to include any embroidered signature or dates then this should be done after the material patch has been cut out. Remove the paper temporarily and pencil on to the fabric what you wish to embroider. In the picture a single strand of Anchor three-stranded cotton was used in a very small chain stitch.

3 Working on a single patch at a time, fold the fabric over one paper edge and pinch along the fold line. Stick the fold down with a small piece of masking tape, and continue in the same way with the other edges all round the patch. Remove the centre pin. Tack the fabric down all round with large stitches and gently remove the masking tape. Iron well. Complete all the patches in this way.

4 Set out your patches in the desired pattern on a large tray beside you. Starting with the centre patch and one that lies beside it, sew the two together where they meet, using fine thread and oversewing with small stitches on the wrong side (taking great care at all the corners). Complete all the sewing and iron well.

Cut the border fabric into four strips and fold lengthwise; half-line them lengthwise with iron-on Vilene. Sew loosely down the edges and iron flat, folding or mitring corners as required. Remove the tacking thread on the patches but leave the papers in place, holding them in position with some short strips of masking tape.

5 To fix the pressed flowers, draw a plan of the patchwork on a large piece of paper and use this as a base on which to arrange the small flowers. Place the pressed blossoms and leaves, etc. on the chart, ensuring that their position is correct. Transfer them carefully to the corresponding place on the material and fix them down with adhesive.

6 To frame up the picture, cut the patchwork to size, using the glass as a cutting guide. Pad lightly before adding the final backing and nailing down.

CARDS AND TAGS

Greetings cards and gift tags decorated with pressed flowers and sent to friends are invariably much appreciated, and this is another area where small flowers can be used most successfully. Greetings cards for

107 A single patch showing a heartsease pansy.

108 A calendar design with flowers mounted on smokey blue card and heat-sealed to protect them (*left*).

109 This calendar has a simple arrangement, covered with transpaseal to protect it (*right*).

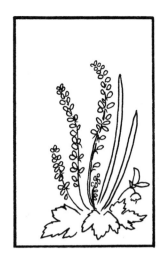

birthdays and anniversaries as well as for Christmas can either be bought ready for use (see list of stockists on p. 118) or easily made from lightweight card.

Measure carefully and remember to cut a card to fit the envelope. Cut cleanly – a guillotine is far better than scissors. You should fold, ornament and ink in any greetings and last of all add your design of wild flowers.

In the three examples on the back jacket you will see cards made with a great variety of tiny florets, buds, leaflets and even half-formed seed-heads. Many plants are represented, including alkanet and may, ling and barren strawberry, cow parsley and nettles, tamaris and speedwell, stitchwort and meadow sweet.

CALENDARS

The two calendars above and on the back jacket are made of strong coloured card. Both are ready for hanging on the wall and have been protected by a plastic skin. One has been heat-sealed and the other has had a layer of sticky-backed plastic laid carefully over everything. Calendars require some protection if they are to last the twelve months.

One of the designs shows some spikes of pennywort and some decorative leaves and grasses to complete the pleasantly-shaped arrangement, while in the second calendar meadow sweet is the dominating flower although a little Japanese knotweet and some grasses extend the range of the subdued colours. The bulky flower on the right of the stalks is an old friend – a pink clover and it has registered its dislike of the press by losing most of its pretty pink!

FLOWERS FROM ABROAD

Wild flowers from other countries in the world often differ greatly from our own in the British Isles and if you can acquire some unusual pressed ones then you will indeed be fortunate. Sometimes they are very like our own, the floral scene in many parts of Europe only differing from

ours because it is so profuse, but some other wild flowers, especially from distant countries lying along different latitudes, can be strange. Sometimes it is in both colour and shape, the shades so bright as to be almost vulgar in tone and the shapes quite bizarre. Our eyes are so attuned to our own indigenous buttercups and daisies that the kangaroo paws and fuzzy bottle brushes of Western Australia and the *Kniphofia rufa* and the *Leonotis leonurus* of South Africa look to us at first sight as if from another planet. But they are frequently very beautiful and, if they are of a shape which will accommodate itself to the flower press, then you will have much to look forward to. Friends going on holiday may be persuaded to press you some but be warned – in many parts of the world it is forbidden to pick wild plants and enquiry should be made. It is possible to buy imported foreign dried flowers, some of which can be pressed a little and used in a design (there is an address in south London where these flowers can be bought included in the list of stockists on p. 118) or, alternatively, you will have to book yourself an extended flowery tour of the world and find your own!

Four pictures have been made to show how varied are some of the wild flowers of the world. Figure 110 shows a small oval design made only from small Alpine flowers picked in the French Alps, not very far from Grenoble. In those high regions you can stand and marvel at the

111 The colours range from palest yellow to purple and a deep, burnt orange-red. It measures 37.5 by 30cm (15 by 12in) and the frame is a good quality modern moulding in grey and gold.

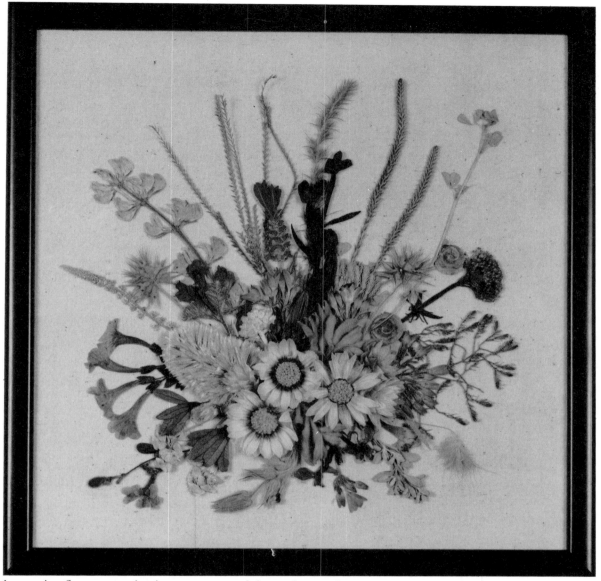

late spring flowers growing in vast carpets of clear colour and you can pick a modest collection of gentians and others and press them to make a picture. The bright shades are retained well, but the diminutive group cannot do full justice to the myriad flowers which grow up on these inhospitable slopes not far from the snow line. The French conservancy regulations forbid any picking from the rarest plants and allow the collection of only 'so many as can be held in one hand' for many others. It is not difficult to find the big coloured posters which show the different categories of these Alpine wild flowers – they are displayed in the information centres and in beauty spots.

The largest of the pictures (*Figure 111*) is of Chilean flowers and this time it is their shape which is so novel. They have been mounted on a

112 The Australian flowers are bright and the strong shade of the blue petals is picked up by the blue frame.

rough linen type material and the creamy shade clearly shows up the unusual outlines. In the third example (*Figure 112*) of non-British flowers you will quickly notice the spikey outline and the papery appearance of some of the petals; this dried material comes from Australia. Quite different from these three designs is the fourth picture, which is made from flowers and leaves picked during a walk along the downs near Winchester at the end of May; they present a gentler group and one that is to us so typically English (see the back jacket illustration and flap).

When you are making pictures and using unusual flowers, always ensure that there is enough space around the design within the frame or mount. Never crowd or cramp an interesting outline – let it stand out boldly and well away from a frame. When you are choosing a moulding for a frame which is to surround a brightly coloured design, always consider using something unusual. The smooth modern frame around the Chilean picture does not detract from the quiet flowing movement of the edging flowers, while the blue painted moulding on the Australian one brings out the similar shade in the papery petals.

Throughout this book you have been encouraged to follow up your work of pressing flowers by learning their names and habits of growth and to understand a little of the world of botany. You will have a considerable collection of identified, pressed flowers mounted on fabric or card by the end of the first year and, since you may not want to make pictures to hang on the wall, to collect them all into an album instead is an ideal way to protect them and to reinforce your new found knowledge.

You will need to buy an album of good quality, but your flowers will merit this expenditure. A finely-made cover and binding will last well and give you pleasure. Figure 14 illustrates just such an album. The pages should be of a colour which will complement the flowers and not overpower the soft shades. You should be able to find an album of this type in shops specialising in paper products, but there are other sorts with high-quality bindings in fabric, leather or card, all of which would suit your collection equally well.

Your Victorian grandmother may well have learnt about wild flowers in this way and your modern album, full of your own preserved flowers, can be a collection to hand on to your grandchildren.

7 History and Classification of Wild Flowers

Every flowering plant in this country belongs to a family, and these families, or 'natural orders' as they used to be called, are simply groupings of similar types of plant. Just as in ethnic groupings, where such races as Japanese, Chinese, Korean and Burmese are all known as Oriental, so in the plant world, similarity of feature makes for a natural grouping. Flower shape, leaf growth, seed formation, all these natural factors are part of the basis for deciding family membership. The much-loved sweet violet is a member of the Violet family, as you would expect, but so too is the small wild pansy, or the heartsease, to give one of its country names. The common dog violet as well as some other less well-known wild violets are also members of this family and all these delicate, pretty plants have similar shaped ovaries where the seeds are formed, a flower with a big lower petal and a spur at the back, and finally seed-capsules which split open into three oval segments to disgorge the ripe seeds. It is having these three factors in common which gives the plants membership of the *Violaceae* family.

The use of Latin dates back many hundreds of years to the days when it was the universal language for scholars and, by its use, information and scholarship could be spread across countries despite the barriers of language and dialect. Knowledge of plants and their properties was extremely important to people in those days – not only to farmers and gardeners but also to herbalists and apothecaries. The primitive medicine which they practised was heavily dependent upon plants; tisanes and concoctions made from powdered roots and seeds, tinctures and lotions from crushed leaves and petals, boiled up potions and even the distillations of oils – the whole business was inextricably entwined with the phases of the moon, folklore and superstition. But, in fact, a tremendous number of plants were used in the medieval treatment of illnesses and wounds and the skills needed in preparing the medicines were handed down very carefully from one generation to the next.

Plants were also the main source for making dyes, which brightened the clothes and household hangings of those days; cosmetics and flavourings for food, too, often came from them and all these things greatly improved the quality of life. This general use of plants to alleviate the diseases and unhappinesses of human beings had a more sinister side, in that there could be found in some plants poisons and

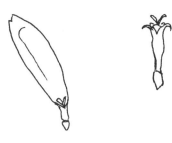

a chamomile

b sneezewort

c yarrow

d coltsfoot

113 Ray and disc type florets.

hallucinogens as well as the soothing and curative compounds. It meant that a precise understanding of plants could bring with it considerable power over simple people who were superstitious, and in many parts of Europe herbal 'cures' were linked with witchcraft.

In every way plants were of vital importance, and scientists were continually seeking to increase their knowledge of them and to perfect the use of their remarkable properties. Ordinary people throughout the land used country names for wild flowers which were familiar to them and these names often varied from one locality to another; but the early scientists and herbalists referred to them by their Latin names and wrote their scholarly books accordingly. In Europe, by the eighteenth century when Linnaeus, a Swedish naturalist, thought out his excellent system of botanical classification, this Latin nomenclature (with some Latinised Greek words included in it) was firmly in use, alongside the country names.

The classification of plants is both simple in idea and effective. It is done in three stages and is based mainly on finding similarities between types of plants and grouping them accordingly, and ultimately on identifying the differences between them and sub-grouping them. Plants which have similar characteristics of flowers or seed containers, and to a lesser extent the leaf and stem formation, are placed in one family; within that group there is then another re-grouping into genus, or kind, by a re-assessment of likeness based on smaller similarities. Finally, the findings of very small differences between plants which to all intents and purposes look the same, leads to another sorting into the smallest category of all, that of species, or special type. By this method, all flowering plants can be listed and classified and everybody in the world, whatever their race or discipline can recognise any plant by name.

All plants, therefore, have their own family name, a Latin name and, for us in the British Isles, the English equivalent. For example, the sweet violet is a member of the *Violaceae*, as has already been mentioned – the Violet family. The Latin name of the plant will always comprise two words: the first, which is always written with a capital letter, will refer to the genus, or kind, and the second word will give the species, or special type. The sweet violet's Latin name is *Viola odorata*; the *Viola* is the genus – a violet – while the second word, *odorata*, means scented or smelling and that specifies the species.

The wild pansy, which is in the same family, has a Latin name *Viola tricolor*: *Viola* again means a violet and *tricolor* means three-coloured (these small flowers are often a combination of three colours – purple, yellow and pale cream). Sometimes you may read in your flower book and notice that a particular flower has a third name, for example *Viola odorata subcarnea* and this informs you that this particular plant is a sub-group or a variety of the sweet violet. The word *subcarnea* refers to the special colour – they are all pink. Plants of one variety, although resembling their cousins in the same species in most ways, will have some minor feature distinct and different. This is normally accounted for by cross fertilisation and the varieties will not necessarily produce seeds which will continue the peculiarity.

Botany is a vast and complicated subject and the classification of flowering plants is only one part of it, and although it would be idle to attempt to explain it fully in a book like this, it would be a pity if it was put to one side and ignored completely. One need make no apology for presenting a simplified explanation of some basic botany; it has been done before – as long ago as 1858 – and by no less an excellent botanist than George Bentham. When he was writing the first introduction to his much read and re-printed *British Flora*, he said that he was writing a description of 'all the plants wild in the British Isles, distinguished by such characters as may be readily perceived by the unlearned eye and expressed as far as lay in my power in ordinary language', and this was because the most expert and kindly Mr Bentham wished to provide a book 'which should enable persons having no previous knowledge of Botany to name the wild flowers they might gather on their country rambles'. People still go rambling and find wild flowers and wish they knew more about them, and the fascination of the subject can be felt by anybody once the basic concepts are outlined and the extraordinary variety and ingenuity of nature used to illustrate them.

a coltsfoot

One of the first flowers which you will be pressing early in the year will be the coltsfoot. The plant belongs to the large Daisy family, the *Compositae*, and there are some 60 other members of this large tribe growing in this country, ranging from the enormous thistle to the humble daisies which invade our lawns. The outstanding feature of *Compositae* is that they are composed of many small florets – each in itself an independent and miniature flower – all clustered together to form a circular flower face. The florets may be either a ray or disc type – the former will have a long, conventional petal while the disc florets are much shorter and stubbier. The ray type can best be seen in the common dandelion, which is made up entirely of this type of floret, while the yellowish-green flower – appropriately called the rayless mayweed – has only the disc type in the flower head. These are the two extremes of type and most other flowers in the family are made up of both; the daisy and the coltsfoot are typical examples and both have a tight cluster of disc florets in the centre of the flower surrounded by a ring of the ray variety which gives a classic and delicate petal-edged appearance (*see Figure 113*).

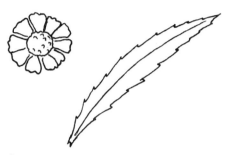

b sneezewort

c daisy

Among the selection of flowers chosen for pressing in this book there are several other members of the *Compositae* family. The chamomile, mugwort, sneezewort and yarrow, as well as the daisy and coltsfoot, all have flower heads composed of small florets. There are very great differences between them so far as the shape of the leaves is concerned, as Figure 114 clearly shows, but it is the composition of the flower heads which determines family membership in this case.

The wild flowers in this book belong to 19 different families between them, some of which are very small and have only a few members. The poppy has a family called after itself and has a few brothers and sisters which grow in the British Isles: the Welsh poppy and the yellow horned poppy, to name two of them, and also the greater celandine. The common factor which determines their family is that they exude a thick milky or coloured sap whenever a part of the plant is broken. The Latin family name is *Paparvaraceae*.

The pretty, pink wild rose is a member of *Rosaceae* – the Rose family – **114**

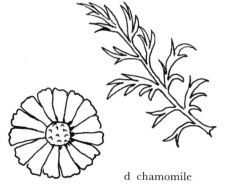

d chamomile

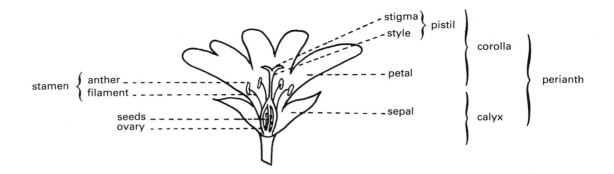

115 Section of a flower.

and it often grows well above head height, clambering up and over hedges, its stems thick and woody and armed with fierce thorns; but the small wild strawberry growing low on the ground with soft and delicate stems is its brother and belongs to the same family. In this case the relationship lies mainly in the shape and constitution of the petals and stamens. Figures 113 and 114 show the similarity of flower between four very different plants, while a comparison of the overall sizes shows the great differences between them.

This method of identification and subsequent classification is part of botany and even to understand a little will give you greater awareness and appreciation of the intricacies of design in common wild flowers. Although many of the families have some easily recognised common factors, some others are grouped together because of a special formation or growth in an obscure part of the plant; for further information of this kind it will be necessary to refer to a botany book on the wild flowers of the British Isles (*see bibliography, p. 118*).

CLASSIFICATION

In the following pages there are short descriptions of the flower families to which the flowers chosen for pressing in this book belong. In each case the notes will describe the distinctive features which are common to all British members of the group – illustrated where necessary – together with any other particularly unusual characteristics. Listed also, on p. 117, will be some of the rare flowers which should not be picked. (You should check these in your botany book for further details.)

The pronunciation of the botanical Latin looks more difficult than it is. The endings of the words often look very bizarre with a motley collection of vowels, but if you remember that 'aceae' simply sounds 'aysee', and 'rae' as 'ree' and 'tae' as 'tee', then half the battle will be won. Break the rest of the word, however long it is, into syllables and, remembering that 'y' sounds as 'i' and the 'c' usually as 'k', you will find that, with a little practice, you will be able to get your tongue round them all! (The bracketed word after the family name may give you some help.)

The following glossary of basic botanical words and the diagram will help you to understand the notes on the flower families.

Annual   A plant which flowers once and lives for one year only
Anther   The part of the stamen where the pollen is formed

Bract   A small leaf which may grow behind the flower or at the joint of a stem

Calyx   The protective covering of a flower – the sepals

Corolla   The whole group of petals which form the flower

Filament   The stalk of a stamen

Ovary   The part at the base of a flower where the seeds are formed

Perennial   A plant which lives for many years and usually flowers every year

Perianth   Petals and sepals together

Petals   The coloured parts of the flower surrounding the stamens and pistil

Pistil   The female part of the flower comprising the ovary, style and stigma

Pollen   Small, often fluffy grains produced in the top of the stamen, each containing a male cell

Sepals   The outer covering which protects the petals when in bud

Stamen   The male part of the flower made up of a filament, anther and the pollen

Stigma   The top of the pistil where the pollen settles – often sticky

Stipule   A small leaf at the base of a leaf stalk

Style   The part between the stigma and the ovary

Ranunculaceae (pronounced 'Ranunkewlaysee') Buttercup family
Flowers for pressing: celandine, meadow buttercup, traveller's joy, wood anemone

One of the most easily identifiable features of this family is the ring of numerous stamens and the fact that most of the flowers are symmetrical. If you look closely into the centre of a buttercup flower which has been open for some time you will see that there are many pistils (these lead down to separate ovaries) and this is another distinctive feature of *Ranunculaceae*. Many flowers in this family are not suitable for pressing, owing to their large size and also to the fact that they often like growing in or close to water – flowers must be completely dry before being put into a press.

Papaveraceae ('Puparvaraysee') Poppy family
Flowers for pressing: field poppy

This is a very small family composed of several types of poppy and the greater celandine. All these plants have in them a distinctive juice which oozes out when ever they are damaged. Sometimes it is milky in appearance but in the case of the greater celandine it is orange and poisonous. These plants also have only two sepals which fall off when the flower opens. Poppies can be difficult to press because of the extreme fragility of their petals – 'backing' is advisable (*see* p. 22).

Violaceae ('Veolaysee') Violet family
Flowers for pressing: common dog violet

This small family of much-loved flowers is characterised by the distinctive corolla of a pansy-style face with a large bottom petal and a spur protruding at the back. The shape of the ovary in violets is always the same, as is the seed-capsule, which splits open into three segments each shaped like a small canoe. The sweet violet, as the name implies, is scented.

Caryophyllaceae ('Karyofilaysee') Pink family
Flowers for pressing: greater stitchwort

It is perhaps the distinctive way in which the leaves grow out from the stem which is the most easily recognisable point about this group of plants. The leaves grow in pairs, direct from the stem and opposite to each other. The flowers usually have five petals, five green sepals and ten stamens.

Malvaceae ('Malvaysee') Mallow family
Flowers for pressing: common mallow

The five-petalled flowers have a protruberant bunch of stamens and the seeds are in round 'cheeses'.

Geraninaceae ('Jeraninaysee') Cranesbill family
Flowers for pressing: herb robert

All members of this family produce very distinctive seed-capsules as the diagram shows. Herb robert is a very common plant, but study the shape of the leaves carefully before you pick specimens for your press – they will be a good guide in final identification. Most of the other plants in this family also have purplish-pink flowers but they are less common and should be left undisturbed. Flowers in this group all have five petals, five sepals and ten stamens and some of the plants with large flowers are very handsome indeed.

Papilionaceae ('Pupilionaysee') Pea family or *Leguminosae*
Flowers for pressing: bird's foot trefoil

There are several well-known plants in this extensive family – gorse and broom to name but two of them – and the shape of the flowers will be familiar to most people. The sepals are joined together in a little green tube at the back of the flower and from this emerge the five petals. The biggest one, which often stands up at the back of the corolla, is called the 'standard'; the two petals at the side are known as the 'wings' and the two at the bottom, which are sometimes partly joined at the lower edge, are the 'keel'. The ten stamens are partly joined together and it is this small tube which ultimately turns into the long pod holding the seeds and which is highly characteristic of the pea family. Pea flowers are difficult to press because of their shape, but the bright coloured flower heads of the bird's foot trefoil retain their rather perky stance very well. Colour of the petals will vary from one area to another, depending upon the type of soil.

Rosaceae ('Roseaysee') Rose family
Flowers for pressing: dog rose, meadow sweet, wild strawberry

There are three very dissimilar plants which all belong to this much varied family: the rambling dog rose, the tall meadow sweet and the low-growing wild strawberry. They have so many differences between them that at first sight it is hard to see why they belong to the same family. They do, however, have two things in common: regular, symmetrical flower heads, usually with five petals and a similar number of sepals, while the stamens are very numerous, and the invariable small stipules which grow at the points at which the proper leaves grow out from the stem.

Onagraceae ('Onagraysee') Willowherb family
Flowers for pressing: rosebay willowherb

The half-a-dozen or so plants in this family enjoy growing in damp places. Rosebay willowherb is a tall, elegant plant with spires of beautiful pink and purple flowers. Each flower is composed of four petals with eight stamens and the rather long ovaries where the seeds eventually form are well below the corolla. This type of flower formation is found in other members of the family with only little variation.

Umbelliferae ('Umbelliferee') Parsley family
Flowers for pressing: cow parsley

This is a very large family with nearly 30 representatives growing in the British Isles. They are very distinctive in appearance because, generally speaking, the mass of tiny florets on the stems grow in a wide-topped cluster which looks like an umbrella. Most of the plants have white flowers and are so similar that it is very difficult to tell one from another; in fact the leaves are probably the best thing to study if you wish to know which plant you have found! Some of these plants are poisonous. Refer to your book on wild flowers for more information.

Ericaceae ('Erikaysee') Heather family
Flowers for pressing: ling

Heathers have one very important thing in common and that is that they all like acid soil conditions and thrive on moors and heathland. The stems are tough and leathery, turning brown in colour when they become old. The leaves are small and needlelike and all members of the family have these characteristics. Most of the flowers appear waxy and papery.

Plumbaginaceae ('Plumbaginaysee') Sea lavender family
Flowers for pressing: thrift

There are few members of this family in the British Isles and thrift, which presses very well, is not so typical – its small flowers are held in a round cluster. The ovary in all these plants makes only one seed despite having five or more stigmas. These plants like growing near the sea.

Primulaceae ('Primulaysee') Primrose family
Flowers for pressing: primrose, cowslip

Both these pretty yellow spring flowers are typical members of this family; they have a corolla of five petals and five stamens and at the back the green sepals are joined together in a long tube.

Boraginaceae ('Boraginaysee') Forget-me-not family
Flowers for pressing: forget-me-not

Members of this family are nearly all hairy and even downright bristly to touch, and the flowers are often blue; they have five petals, five sepals and five stamens. The flowers are in little heads which slowly uncurl as the small florets open.

Labiatae ('Laybeeaytee') Deadnettle family
Flowers for pressing: wild thyme

The small, low-growing plant, wild thyme, is a member of this large family and has over 30 relations growing in this country. The stems of all the plants in the family are square and the leaves grow in pairs opposite to each other on the stem. A strong scent (either pleasant or acrid) is also a firm characteristic of *Labiatae* plants, and in the case of the wild thyme it is very agreeable.

Rubiaceae ('Rubeeaysee') Bedstraw family
Flowers for pressing: lady's bedstraw

The leaves of these often delicate-looking plants grow out from the stem in small rings or whorls and in each group there will only be two real leaves – the others, which may well look very similar, will only be enlarged stipules. This unusual leaf formation is a most distinctive feature of bedstraw plants.

Dipsacaceae ('Dipsukaysee') Scabious family
Flowers for pressing: devil's bit scabious

The great teasel, which can grow up to 2m (78in) in height, has the same special features in its flower head as does the small blue scabious – there are dozens of small florets clustered together in the flower heads – and this makes both members of *Dipsacaceae*.

Compositae ('Kompositee') Daisy family
Flowers for pressing: chamomile, coltsfoot, daisy, mugwort, sneezewort, yarrow, ox-eye daisy

This is one of the best-known families in the plant world because the common or garden daisy belongs to it. But it is the composition of the flower heads which give the first main characteristic; they are made up of many small florets of which there are two types: a disc type, such as are found in the yellow centre of a daisy, and a ray type, which have a single petal and, in the example of the daisy, form the white frilly edge. Each of the florets is a separate little flower in itself and ultimately turns into a seed; dispersal is usually helped by the wind, which catches the silken 'umbrella' to which the seed is fastened.

Amaryllidaceae ('Amerillidaysee') Daffodil family
Flowers for pressing: snowdrop

The well-known daffodil is a member of this family, along with the snowdrop, and both of them have a 'trumpet' surrounding the stamens. The ovary is behind the flower and the seeds form in the three sections of it.

Cucurbitaceae ('Kewkurbitaysee') Cucumber family
Flowers for pressing: white bryony

The white bryony is the only member of this family growing in Britain. The plants have both male and female flowers and strong tendrils with which they hold themselves safely aloft as they grow upwards. In the case of the white bryony, it can reach the top of the hedges easily.

Glossary

Wild Flowers

agrimony (*Agrimonia eupatoria*)
Small yellow flowers grow on spikes – choose the shortest and press whole. Leaves too are useful. *June to August*

alkanet, green (*Pentaglottis sempervirens*)
Blue can fade in old flowers – detach a few and press hard, also small clusters of buds. *May to July*

Alpine lady's mantle
see lady's mantle

anemone, wood (*Anemone nemorosa*)
See p. 62

angelica (*Angelica sylvestris*)
See umbelliferae

asphodel, bog (*Narthecium ossifragum*)
Short spires of yellow flowers which turn reddish when old. *July to September*

autumn squill
See squill

barren strawberry
See strawberry

bedstraw, hedge (*Galium mollugo*)
Press pieces of stem complete with clusters of white flowers and leaves – they dry dark green or black. *June to September*

bedstraw, lady's (*Galium verum*)
See p. 49

bell heather
See heather

bellflower, nettle-leaved (*Campanula trachelium*)
Take one or two blue flowers from a stem. Tend to fade. *July to September*

betony (*Stachys officinalis*)
The pink flower heads can be pressed whole and the leaves have well-serrated edges. *June to September*

bird's foot trefoil (*Lotus corniculatus*)
See p. 36

bistort (*Polygonum bistorta*)
Use young pink flower spikes before they open fully. *May to August*

bitter vetch
See vetch

black medick
See medick

bladder campion (*Silene cucubalus*)
See campion

bluebell (*Endymion non-scriptus*)	Pick freshly opened flower stems only. Pick off fully opened flowers and press separately from the stem and its tip of buds. Re-assemble when dry. Requires tight pressing. *May to June*
blue-eyed Mary (*Omphalodes verna*)	A garden plant often found naturalised in woods. Detach bright blue flowers and press by themselves. Put together with stem and leaves after dry. Colour may be fugitive. *March to May*
bog asphodel	*See* asphodel
borage (*Borago officinalis*)	Detach blue flowers first from the dark bud clusters, press both. *June to September*
bramble – blackberry (*Rubus fruticosus*)	The leaves are well worth pressing. Avoid the old ones and look for them in the autumn when they first turn deep red. Flowers difficult – small sprays of grey buds press well but are bulky.
broom (*Sarothamnus scoparius*)	Newly opened yellow flowers press well in profile – foliage tends to dry brown or black. Use tips of stems. *May and June*
bryony – white	*See* white bryony
bugle (*Ajuga reptans*)	These tight little flower heads of blue-purple florets press well – remember to pick the leaves too. *May to July*
buttercup, bulbous (*Ranunculous bulbosus*)	Familiar flowers on graceful stems – they press well. *April to June*
buttercup, creeping (*Ranunculus repens*)	Press the yellow flowers, buds and small seed-heads. The leaves have pale spots on them. *May to August*
buttercup, meadow	*See* p. 74
campion, bladder (*Silene cucubalus*)	The buds and calyx are a silvery green, veined and very attractive when pressed. *June to September*
campion, sea (*Silene maritima*)	Fairly common on shingle beaches. Pick the buds and white flowers sparingly. The calyx is veined with brown. *June to September*
campion, white and red (*Melandrium album, Melandrium rubrum*)	Difficult to press – always select the newly opened flowers for pressing. *May to August*
cat's ear (*Hypochoaris radicata*)	Pick and press the bright yellow flowers and the buds in profile – choose the smallest. *May to September*
celandine, lesser (*Ranunculus ficaria*)	*See* p. 50
centaury, common (*Centaurium minus*)	The small pink flowers and buds are useful. *July to September*

chamomile (*Chamaemelum nobile*); chamomile, corn (*Anthemis arvensis*); chamomile, stinking (*Anthemis cotula*)	Use the freshly opened daisy-shaped flowers for pressing – a blotting paper 'collar' may help (*See p. 22*). The old flowers with turned back petals and deep golden central boss will not press. Small buds and leaves are also useful. For corn chamomile see p. 80. *June to September*
cinquefoil, creeping (*Potentilla reptans*)	The yellow petals of these flowers tend to drop off in the press – handle carefully. Leaves are silvery underneath and very useful. *June to September*
coltsfoot (*Tussilago farfara*)	*See* p. 38
columbine (*Aquilegia vulgaris*)	The flowers press well in profile only, pink, white or purple; try the buds too. *May and June*
comfrey (*Symphytum officinale*)	Profile pressing only for both purple and cream varieties – the latter dry darker. *May to June*
common centaury	*See* centaury
common fumitory	*See* fumitory
common mallow	*See* mallow
common melilot	*See* melilot
common milkwort	*See* milkwort
common St John's wort	*See* St John's wort
common vetch	*See* vetch
corn chamomile	*See* chamomile
corn poppy	*See* poppy
cornflower (*Centaurea cyanus*)	Use small flowers, the bright blue florets can be used separately, the colour is excellent. One flower head goes a long way, so pick sparingly. *June to August*
cow parsley (*Anthriscus sylvestris*)	*See* p. 75 and umbelliferae
cow-wheat (*Melampyrum pratense*)	The small yellow and cream flowers are un-distinguished but the sharp leaves and buds dry black. *May to September*
cowslip (*Primula veris*)	*See* p. 42
creeping buttercup	*See* buttercup
creeping Jenny (*Lysimachia nummularia*)	Press the stems complete with the hanging yellow globes – rather delicate. *June to August*
cross-leaved heath (*Erica tetralix*)	*See* heath
cudweed, marsh (*Filanginella uliginosum*)	Dry, little yellow flowers which grow in clusters, they press well, as do the silvery-grey leaves. *July to August*
daisy (*Bellis perennis*)	*See* p. 74

daisy, ox-eye	*See* ox-eye daisy
devil's bit scabious (*Succisa pratensis*)	*See* scabious
dog rose (*Rosa canina*)	*See* p. 44
dog's mercury (*Mercurialis perennis*)	The small spikes of green flowers are useful. *February to April*
dropwort (*Filipendula vulgaris*)	The leaves are beautiful and delicate – press carefully. The cream flowers are similar to those of meadow sweet but not as good. *June to August*
eyebright (*Euphrasia officinalis*)	Small sprigs of combined flowers and leaves can be pressed, but the flowers are very small. *June to September*
green alkanet (*Pentaglottis sempervirens*)	*See* alkanet
fat hen (*Chenopodium album*)	Pick small spikes of the greenish-grey flowers and small dark leaves. *July to September*
fennel (*Foeniculum vulgare*)	*See* umbelliferae
feverfew (*Tanacetum parthenium*)	Very useful little 'daisy' flowers. Press buds, flowers and leaves. *July and August*
field scabious	*See* scabious
fleabane (*Pulicaria dysenterica*)	Press these bright yellow flowers full-face and give them plenty of room on the blotting paper. Use the buds too and small leaves which are heavily veined. *July to September*
flowering rush	*See* rush
forget-me-not, water (*Myosotis palustris*)	This forget-me-not has got larger flowers than the one chosen for Figure 78, but it will also press well; lay the complete stems with the curled tips of buds head to tail in the press. *April to September*
fuchsia (*Fuchsia megallanica*)	The hanging red flowers and dark stamens press very well. Pick the tips of stems with buds and small leaves. *June to September*
fumitory, common (*Fumaria officinalis*)	Small clusters of pale pink florets tipped with dark purple should be placed carefully on the blotting paper. Leaves are delicate too – get this plant into press quickly. *May to October*
fumitory, ramping (*Fumaria capreolata*)	Treat as the common fumitory
germander speedwell	*See* speedwell
geum (*Geum rivale*)	The neat hanging heads of this graceful plant are pinkish-brown. Seed-heads press well too. *May to September*

108

goldenrod (*Solidago virgaurea*)	Small bunches of yellow florets and buds can be pressed as well as the lanceolate leaves. *July to September*
gorse (*Ulex europaeus*)	Select small flowers or buds in profile only. *April to June*
great willowherb	*See* willowherb
greater knapweed	*See* knapweed
green alkanet	*See* alkanet
groundsel (*Senecio vulgaris*)	Buds, flowers, and seed-heads all press very well. *January to December*
hairy tare (*Vicia hirsuta*)	Use the leaves only – the tiny tendrils are unusual.
hawkweed (*Compositae*)	The smallest flowers only should be chosen for pressing from plants in this large family of hawkweeds and hawksbits – mouse-ear hawkweed has attractive red sepals.
heartsease	*See* pansy, wild
heath, cross-leaved (*Erica tetralix*)	This heather has pink bells and presses well. As with all heathers handle carefully when dry. *July to September*
heather, or ling (*Calluna vulgaris*)	*See* p. 47
heather, bell (*Erica cinerea*)	Red-purple bells on leafy spikes – avoid the very large ones. Search for plants with dark bronzey foliage. *June to September*
hedge bedstraw	*See* bedstraw
hedge woundwort	*See* woundwort
herb robert (*Geranium robertianum*)	*See* p. 77
hoary plantain	*See* plantain
hogweed (*Heracleum sphondylium*)	*See* umbelliferae
honeysuckle (*Lonicera periclymenum*)	Creamy trumpet-shaped flowers held in clusters. Scented. Pick small ones newly opened. *June to October*
hop (*Humulus lupulus*)	The green female flowers press very well, as do the leaves. *July to August*
hop trefoil (*Trifolium campestre*)	The small yellow flowers are best pressed in clusters. *May to August*
ivy (*Hedera helix*)	Use the small leaves and partially formed seed-heads; search for bronze and green bi-coloured leaves, especially in winter.
ivy-leafed toadflax (*Cymbalaria muralis*)	Very delicate prostrate plants. Pick and press whole stems complete with leaves, and tiny lilac and yellow flowers. *April to November*

kidney vetch	*See* vetch
knapweed, greater (*Centaurea scabiosa*)	Look for the small flowers and buds; the strong mauve shade is retained well. Leaves have strange indentations. *July to September*
knapweed, lesser (*Centaurea nigra*)	As for the common knapweed – ensure that the bulky mauve heads are tightly pressed. *June to September*
lady's bedstraw	*See* p. 49 and bedstraw
lady's mantle (*Alchemilla vulgaris*)	The flowers are green and very small, the leaves are an unusual shape and useful. *June to September*
lady's mantle, Alpine (*Alchemilla alpina*)	Press small clusters of the green flowers and also the leaves which are silver-grey underneath. *May to September*
lady's smock (*Cardamine pratensis*)	The pink flowers are difficult to press when fully out but the tips of the flowering stems and buds can be useful in designs. *April to June*
lavender, sea (*Limonium vulgare*)	The papery mauve and white flowers are excellent. Take small sprays. *July to September*
lesser celandine (*Ranunculus ficaria*)	*See* p. 50
lesser knapweed	*See* knapwed
lesser periwinkle	*See* periwinkle
loostrife, yellow (*Lysimachia vulgaris*)	Detach yellow flowers and press full-face. *July to August*
mallow, common (*Malva sylvestris*)	*See* p. 71
marguerite	*See* ox-eye daisy
marjoram (*Origanun vulgare*)	The small sprigs of pink florets and darker sepals as well as the leaves dry well. *July to September*
marsh cudweed	*See* cudweed
marsh woundwort	*See* woundwort
mayweed, scentless (*Matricaria maritima*)	The white 'daisy' flowers have green centres when first out. Use a 'collar' if necessary. Leaves are fine fronds and useful. *July to September*
meadow buttercup	*See* p. 74 and buttercup
meadow sweet (*Filipendula ulmaria*)	*See* p. 83
marsh thistle	*See* thistle
medick, black (*Medicago lupulina*)	Small yellow flowers of clover-shape. Press small seed-heads too. *April to August*
melilot, white (*Melilotus alba*)	The sharp spike of white flowers dry well. *May to September*

melilot, yellow (*Melilotus officinalis*)	Both flower spikes and leaves press well. *June to September*
mint water (*Mentha aquatica*)	Choose the young flowering side spikes for pressing. *July to September* (Other wild mints can also provide similar material for your press.)
milkwort (*Polygala vulgaris*)	Pick small stems of these blue flowers using scissors. Excellent for colour. *June to August*
montbretia (*Crocosmia*)	These bright orange flowers are probably escapees from gardens which have naturalised themselves. Pick spikes of flowers and buds and press whole without trimming. They hold their colour well. *July to August*
mouse-ear hawkweed	*See* hawkweed
mugwort (*Artemisia vulgaris*)	*See* p. 69
mullein (*Verbascum thapsus*)	These tall plants are much too large to press whole – carefully detach a few of the yellow flowers and some silvery hirsute leaves. *June to August*
nettle, stinging (*Urtica dioica*)	Hanging tassles of tiny green flowers. Press small leaves and flowers. Beware the hairs! *June to September*
nettle-leaved bellflower	*See* bellflower
nipplewort (*Lapsana communis*)	Both buds and yellow flowers press well. *June to August*
ox-eye daisy (*Chrysanthemum leucanthemum*)	*See* p.76
pansy- wild or heartsease (*Viola tricolor*)	The flowers can be a mixture of yellow, purple and cream. Trim stalk away from behind corolla. *April to September*
parsley, cow	*See* p. 75 and umbelliferae
pennywort (*Umbilicus rupestris*)	Common in the West Country, the pale greenish flower spikes press quite well – rather succulent, they will require time to dry properly. *May to August*
pepper saxifrage	*See* umbelliferae
periwinkle, lesser (*Vinca minor*)	These low-growing plants are often found in gardens as well as in the wild; press the blue flowers. *March to May*
persicaria (*Polygonum persicaria*)	Pick the pink-tipped flower stalks when they are young. The leaves have a single black splodge on them. *June to October*

pineapple weed, or rayless mayweed (*Chamomilla suaveolens*)	Small flowers and buds when young and in profile only; green and unusual shape. *June to September*
plantain, hoary (*Plantago media*)	Take the long stems before the florets open. Leaves are rounded, dark and effective. *May to August*
poppy, corn (*Papaver rhoeas*)	See p. 80
primrose (*Primula vulgaris*)	See p. 72
ragwort (*Senecio jacobaea*)	Untidy yellow flowers but they can be useful if pressed in profile. *June to October*
ramping fumitory	*See* fumitory
ramsons (*Allium ursinum*)	Detach the delicate white flowers and press separately. *April to June*
raspberry, wild (*Rubus idaeus*)	Leaves only – the undersides are a beautiful silver-grey
red campion	*See* campion
rose, wild	*See* p. 44
rosebay willowherb	*See* p. 53 and willowherb
rush, flowering (*Butomus umbellatus*)	Cut a few of the pink florets from each flower head. *July to September*
St John's wort, common (*Hypericum perforatum*)	Star-shaped yellow flowers press very well – also the sprigs of bud. *July to September*
St John's wort, slender (*Hypericum pulchrum*)	Tinged with red, this plant provides good material, especially the buds. *July to September*
scarlet pimpernel (*Anagallis arvensis*)	Tiny scarlet flowers are hard to press – handle them with great care when they are dry. *May to October*
scabious, devil's bit (*Succisa pratensis*)	See p. 69
scabious, field (*Knautia arvensis*)	Pick the smallest flowers on the long stems when the colour blue will be strongest – also buds and deeply indented leaves. *June to September*
scabious, small (*Scabiosa columbaria*)	Make sure you only use freshly opened flower heads – the blue fades in old flowers. *June to August*
scentless mayweed (*Matricaria maritima*)	*See* mayweed
sea campion	*See* campion
sea lavender	*See* lavender
shepherd's purse (*Capsella bursa-pastoris*)	Press the small seed-heads only – traditional 'purse' shape. *All the year round*

silverweed (*Potentilla anserina*)	The yellow flowers tend to loose their petals when drying. The leaves are excellent – undersides are silver. *July to August*
small scabious	*See* scabious
sneezewort (*Achillea ptarmica*)	*See* p. 65
snowdrop (*Galanthus nivalis*)	*See* p. 54
sorrel, sheep's (*Rumex acetosella*)	These familiar red spikes growing in the grass press excellently. Choose ones that are just out. *May to August*
speedwell, germander (*Veronica chamaedrys*)	Pick the tops of the stems with the clusters of buds, blue flowers and small leaves – sadly the blue will often fade when drying. (All the speedwells are delicate and unsatisfactory to use.) *March to July*
spurge, wood (*Euphorbia amygdaloides*)	Small clusters of bright green flowers and leaves. (Other members of the family will also provide suitable material.) *April to May*
squill, autumn (*Scilla autumnalis*)	Locally common but pick very sparingly using scissors. Blue. *July to September*
stinging nettle (*Urtica dioica*)	*See* nettle
stinking chamomile	*See* chamomile
stitchwort, greater (*Stellaria holostea*)	*See* p. 77
strawberry, barren (*Potentilla sterilis*)	Leaves only – they are an unusual bluish-green
strawberry, wild (*Fragaria vesca*)	*See* p. 66
sundew (*Drosera rotundifolia*)	The tips of the tiny flowering spikes hang over; they dry well. Pick them carefully. *June to August*
sweet violet (*Viola odorata*)	*See* violet
tansy (*Tanacetum vulgare*)	The stubby bright yellow flowers press well with heavy pressure – the leaves too are good. *July to September*
thistle, marsh (*Cirsium palustre*)	Growing on moors and boglands these thistles are often small enough to press satisfactorily. Reddish-purple in shade. (Space out well on blotting paper as with all thistles and their leaves.) *June to August*
thistle, welted (*Carduus acanthoides*)	When small, the leaves are very useful in pictures.

thrift (*Armeria maritima*)	*See* p. 78
thyme, wild (*Thymus drucei*)	*See* p. 60
toadflax, ivy-leafed	*See* ivy-leafed toadflax
traveller's joy (*Clematis vitalba*)	*See* p. 57
tufted vetch	*See* vetch
umbelliferae	A large family. Flower heads are clustered in umbrella shapes. Usually white. Identification can be difficult; shape of leaf and height of plant are useful here.
vetch	A very large family. The small typical pea-shaped flowers are difficult to press but worth the effort. Leaves sometimes have tendrils and press very well.
violet (*Viola riviniana*)	*See* p. 41
violet, sweet (*Viola odorata*)	The little flowers may be either blue or white and, although they tend to fade when drying, their unusual shape is useful in pictures, as are their heart-shaped leaves. *February to April*
water forget-me-not	*See* forget-me-not
water mint	*See* mint
welted thistle	*See* thistle
wheat, cow-	*See* cow-wheat
white bryony (*Bryonia dioica*)	*See* p. 58
white melilot	*See* melilot
wild pansy	*See* pansy
wild raspberry	*See* raspberry
wild rose	*See* p. 44
wild strawberry	*See* p. 66
wild thyme	*See* p. 60
willowherb, great (*Epilobium hirsutum*)	Pink flowers and buds press well. *July and August*
willowherb, rosebay (*Epilobium angustifolium*)	*See* p. 53
wood anemone	*See* p. 62
wood spurge	*See* spurge
woody nightshade or bittersweet (*Solanum dulcamara*)	The small hanging clusters of purple and yellow flowers and buds press very well. *May to August*
wormwood (*Artemisia absinthium*)	The creamy-grey flowers grow on spikes and press very well indeed, as do the leaves. *July and August*
woundwort, hedge (*Stachys sylvatica*)	Spikes of reddish-mauve flowers should be pressed whole. Leaves notched – a good shape. *May to August*

woundwort, marsh (*Stachys palustris*)	The mauve-pink florets are clustered together – choose the smaller ones and press tightly. *July to September*
yarrow (*Achillea millefolium*)	*See* p. 67
yellow melilot	*See* melilot
yellow loosestrife	*See* loosestrife

Trees

A number of trees have flowers, leaves and even seeds which are suitable material for pressing and the following list may be helpful

alder (*Alnus glutinosa*)	Catkins *February to March*
beech (*Fagus sylvatica*)	Leaves – especially when small and young. The untidy flowers can also be pressed
beech, copper	As above
crab apple (*Malus*)	Buds of the pink and white flowers in *April and May*
elder (*Sambucus nigra*)	Both flowers and buds are excellent – a creamy shade. *June and July*
English oak (*Quercus robur*)	Only the small leaves and the green flower tassles can be used in most pictures. *April to May*
guelder rose (*Viburnum opulus*)	Between a small tree and a shrub – the white flowers press well. *May to July*
hawthorn or may (*Crataegus monogyna*)	Small clusters of pink or white flowers. *May and June* Leaves in spring and also, when coloured, in the autumn
hazel (*Corylus avellana*)	Catkins and small leaves. *January to March*
hornbeam (*Carpinus betulus*)	Unusual catkins, the tips of twigs with small emerging leaves and the seeds all press well. *April and May*
lime (*Tilia*)	The buds and flowers are excellent. *July*
poplar, grey (*Populus canescens*)	The undersides of the leaves are silvery-grey
silver birch (*Betula pendula*)	Small leaves and catkins. *April and May*
tamarisk (*Tamarix anglica*)	Small fronds of leaf and flowers. *June to September*
wayfaring tree (*Viburnum lantana*)	Creamy white flowers and wrinkled leaves. *April to June*
wild cherry (*Prunus avium*)	Flowers and small leaves. *April and May*
willow (*Salix*)	Many of the silver-leaved willows provide beautiful material for your press

Miscellaneous

ferns	Most ferns press well and offer very useful material for your pictures. The hart's tongue, *Phyllitis vulgare* is disappointing and tends to lose its green colour.
grasses	Grasses, members of the *Gramineae* family nearly all press and dry well. Pick them early when the heads first break open. To achieve pale golden grass stems, pick and press when young and bleach in the sun after drying.
lichens	Pick small tufts of lichen and ensure they are fairly dry before putting in the press. Most types press well.
mosses	Experiment with pressing mosses – small pieces of feathery types often keep their colour well. There are many different types of moss.
rushes	Members of the *Juncaceae* family usually provide good material for pressing – remember to pick the stems when the flowers first break open.
sedges	The smaller members of the *Cyperaceae* family will press well and be useful in your pictures.

Protected Flora

The Wildlife and Countryside Act of 1981 makes it an offence to pick or damage any part of the protected flora on the list or to uproot them, without a special licence. It is also an offence to uproot and remove any plant growing on private land without the permission of the owner or his tenant. There are certain areas in the British Isles which are designated Conservation Areas and here too you are not allowed to pick flowers and their leaves.

Adder's tongue spearwort (*Ranunculus ophioglossifolius*)
Alpine catchfly (*Lychnis alpina*)
Alpine gentian (*Gentiana nivalis*)
Alpine sow-thistle (*Cicerbita alpina*)
Alpine woodsia (*Woodsia alpina*)
Bedstraw broomrape (*Orobanche caryophyllacea*)
Blue heath (*Phyllodoce caerulea*)
Brown galingale (*Cyperus fuscus*)
Cheddar pink (*Dianthus gratianopolitanus*)
Childling pink (*Petroraghia nanteuilii*)
Diapensia (*Diapensia lapponica*)
Dickie's bladder fern (*Cystopteris dickieana*)
Downy woundwort (*Stachys germanica*)
Drooping saxifrage (*Saxifraga cernua*)
Early spider orchid (*Ophrys sphegodes*)
Fen orchid (*Liparis loeselii*)
Fen violet (*Viola persicifolia*)
Field cow-wheat (*Melampyrum arvense*)
Field eryngo (*Eryngium campestre*)
Field wormwood (*Artemisia campestris*)
Ghost orchid (*Epipogium aphyllum*)

Greater yellow-rattle (*Rhinanthus serotinus*)
Jersey cudweed (*Gnaphalium luteoalbum*)
Killarney fern (*Trichomanes speciosum*)
Lady's slipper (*Cypripedium calceolus*)
Late spider orchid (*Ophrys fuciflora*)
Least lettuce (*Lactuca saligna*)
Limestone woundwort (*Stachys alpina*)
Lizard orchid (*Himantoglossum hircinum*)
Mezereon (*Daphne mezereum*)
Military orchid (*Orchis militaris*)
Monkey orchid (*Orchis simia*)
Norwegian sandwort (*Arenaria norvegica*)
Oblong woodsia (*Woodsia ilvensis*)
Oxtongue broomrape (*Orobanche loricata*)
Perennial knawel (*Scleranthus perennis*)
Plymouth pear (*Pyrus cordata*)
Purple spurge (*Euphorbia peplis*)
Red helleborine (*Cephalanthera rubra*)
Ribbon-leaved water-plantain (*Alisma gramineum*)
Rock cinquefoil (*Potentilla rupestris*)
Rough marsh-mallow (*Althaea hirsuta*)

Round-headed leek (*Allium sphaerocephalon*)
Sea knotgrass (*Polygonum maritimum*)
Sea lavender (*Limonium paradoxum/ Limonium recurvum*)
Sickle-leaved hare's-ear (*Bupleurum falcatum*)
Small alison (*Alyssum alyssoides*)
Small hare's-ear (*Bupleurum baldense*)
Snowdon lily (*Lloydia serotina*)
Spiked speedwell (*Veronica spicata*)
Spring gentian (*Gentiana verna*)
Starfruit (*Damasonium alisma*)
Starved wood-sedge (*Carex depauperata*)
Teesdale sandwort (*Minuartia stricta*)
Thistle broomrape (*Orobanche reticulata*)
Triangular club-rush (*Scirpus triquetrus*)
Tufted saxifrage (*Saxifraga cespitosa*)
Water germander (*Teucrium scordium*)
Whorled solomon's-seal (*Polygonatum verticillatum*)
Wild cotoneaster (*Cotoneaster integerrimus*)
Wild gladiolus (*Gladiolus illyricus*)

Bibliography

Richard and Alistair Fitter and Marjorie Blamey, *The Wild Flowers of Britain and Northern Europe* (Collins, 1974)

W. Keble Martin, *Concise British Flora in Colour* (Michael Joseph and Ebury Press, 1965)

B.E. Nicholson, S. Ary and M. Gregory, *The Oxford Book of Wild Flowers* (Oxford University Press, 1960)

Roger Phillips, *Wild Flowers of Britain* (Pan Books and Ward Lock, 1977)

Reader's Digest, *Field Guide to the Wild Flowers of Britain* (Reader's Digest Association, 1981)

List of Suppliers

Wild flower seeds

Suffolk Herbs
Sawyers Farm
Little Cornard
Sudbury
Suffolk

Dried flower importers

Machin and Henry Ltd
Unit 102, Building B
Faircharm Trading Estate
Creekside
London SE8

Frame makers and heat-sealing specialists

Arthur Harding
The Old Bakery
High Cross
Nr Ware
Herts

Paper products

Impress Cards
Slough Farm
Westhall
Halesworth
Suffolk

Paperchase
213 Tottenham Court Road
London W1

Index